WAR

OR

PEACE

AVOID THE DESTRUCTION OF DIVORCE COURT

BY JORYN JENKINS

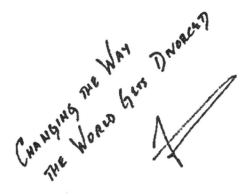

Changing the Way The World Gets Divorced

OPEN PALM PRESS

This is a work based on actual clients and dissolutions of marriage. I have tried to recreate events and conversations from my memories of them. Names and identifying details have been changed to protect the privacy of the individuals involved.

Although the author and publisher have made every effort to ensure that the information in this book was correct at press time, the author and publisher do not assume and hereby disclaim any liability to any party for any loss, damage, or disruption caused by errors or omissions, whether such errors or omissions result from negligence, accident, or any other cause.

WAR OR PEACE

Published by Open Palm Press
Copyright © 2014 by Joryn Jenkins.
Cover art by Shake Creative

First Printing: September 2014
Printed in the United States of America

First Edition: September 2014

Dedication

I dedicate this book to the many who seek a peaceful and diplomatic conclusion to certain relationships. May you each find the cooperative or collaborative path to the ending of one union, and to the beginning of the rest of your life.

Acknowledgements

This book was a long time in the writing. The war stories came first. Thirty-four years' worth. They are like the car accidents that compel all of us rubberneckers to slow down to take a gander at. We are all so grateful that it's not us the paramedics are working on by the side of the road.

So, too, in the world of divorce, where well over 50% of us are likely to be that guy lying on the stretcher, that husband enjoined from going back home by the judge because he posted a stupid comment on Facebook, or that wife who lost one night a week with her kids because she kept taking photos of their new boo-boos when they came home from visiting their dad.

I always felt compelled to record these "war story" experiences, often because they were so hard to believe.

It was only recently that I realized that I could make a bigger difference than just one client at a time, that if people understood, *before* they consulted a divorce lawyer, that they have choices in the divorce process, the world (at least, the one in which *I* live, along with so many confronted by divorce) would be a better place.

So I must first thank all of my courtless and collaborative clients who, over the years, made the right choices, despite that they invariably struggled to ensure that the dissolution of each of their marriages was peaceful. It was never easy for any of them. But they trusted me. And they have taught me so much. They provided the stories that evidence the lights at the end of their many tunnels.

I must thank one of my clients, Jan Powell, in particular. During the dissolution of her marriage, we became good friends. She not only chose the courtless divorce option, but she also edited the entire manuscript for this book, and, in the process, helped me to become a better writer and a more skilled communicator.

I must also acknowledge all of the collaborative professionals with whom I and my clients have worked over the years. They toiled to brainstorm and problem solve the hard issues; they modelled the right behaviors; and they helped me show our clients how both to identify interests and also to separate those interests from positions. Most crucial, they worked with me to tutor our clients on how to negotiate their interests without giving in, but also without waging war. I have learned much from them, as well.

It goes without saying that I thank Stu Webb, Pauline Tesler, and Norma Trusch, as well as Woody Mosten, Enid Miller-Ponn, Robert Merlin, and Rosemarie Roth, among many other mentors, for leading the way for both me and the rest of us who are now committed to the collaborative way. They all understood early on that families do not belong in the courtroom.

Pauline Tesler, in particular, shared a particularly poignant story with me that I have included here. Alice Boullosa, Robert Kokol, and Mark Baer also contributed their time, their insights, and some powerfully motivating anecdotes.

Then, too, I must thank my staff, who work with me daily on our own cases. Sheila Fickes, Marissa Rozas, Brie Zupko, and Alex Tsavaris were an intrinsic part of the team that made this book a reality. But Lori Skipper, especially, was a huge asset; not only is she a compassionate healer in her own right, but she also helped me both with the substantive work of explaining the various processes, as well as with distilling our clients' stories into the vibrant tales you read in this book.

Gary Teaney, my business consultant, brought more expertise to our table than I ever dreamed possible. Not only did he share his personal war story, but this book would never have come to fruition without his active listening skills.

I am very grateful to my husband, Todd Jones, and to our daughter, Alexis Kiri Jones, for their support, encouragement, and constructive feedback. This book is a better book because of them.

Finally, I thank *Next Generation Divorce*, my collaborative practice group, and its president, Adam Cordover, for our members' consistent willingness to consider new ideas and to provide me with constant inspiration. I can't begin to name every NGD member who has motivated me to complete this task, but you know who you are. Thank you all so much.

What Others Are Saying About This Book...

"Joryn Jenkins' new book, *War or Peace (Avoid the Destruction of Divorce Court)*, adds to the growing literature of Collaborative Divorce practice, a lively, client-centered guide focusing on the significant advantages of a collaborative team divorce — and the significant risks of choosing a less family-centric process for moving through the breakup and recovery process. While it is not meant to replace more comprehensive guides to the collaborative process or to the professional makeup of a full interdisciplinary collaborative team, the book speaks powerfully to clients at the emotional level – where divorce-related decisions are most often made – through vividly written accounts of how real people moving through divorce made good and not-so-good process choices, and where those choices led them. The particular power of this book lies in its rich narratives of the potential for grace and healing that collaborative practice offers to couples willing to embrace its tenets."

- **Pauline Tesler, Co-Founder and first President, *International Academy of Collaborative Professionals*, and Director, *Integrative Law Institute at Commonweal***

"Joryn Jenkins has taken all of the mystery and confusion out of the divorce process and made it manageable and understandable for the client contemplating the end of a marriage. Most helpful are the examples she gives from her own experience as a respected 34-year lawyer and mediator. *War or Peace* should be on the shelf of every family lawyer. The book's description of the various roads to divorce is the most complete and accurate I have read and I plan to share it with all of my new clients. Thank you, Joryn, for your work as a peacemaker. This book is just the latest in a long line of contributions you have made to the practice of family law."

- **Norma Trusch, Collaborative Lawyer, Former President of the *International Academy of Collaborative Professionals*, and Member, *Lone Star Collaborative Training***

"Oftimes someone facing divorce comes to it — based on recommendations from well-meaning friends, family, even professionals — with more than enough fear about what *might* happen if they are not excessive in their demands, aggressive in insisting they have 'rights' to some specific outcome, resistant to any concessions, and/or insistent upon punishment of the other person who's 'fault' it is that any of this is happening. In *War or Peace*, Joryn Jenkins has done a fine job of giving people insight into what *will* happen if they follow such a path, as well as how the collaborative practice process can support a divorcing couple in having discussions and reaching decisions that will actually meet their needs, and not just respond to their fears. Using general information, as well as a collection of tales that range from 'Dear God!' horrible to 'Aawww' heartwarming, Joryn has presented a volume here that anyone contemplating, facing, or going through a divorce should definitely read to get a valuable sense on how, and why, to avoid slash and burn warfare."

> **- carl Michael rossi, Collaborative Lawyer, *Collaborative Practice Chicago*, Co-Editor, *The World of Collaborative Practice***

"Anyone considering a divorce can certainly learn from [this] book how the divorce process works, in court and out of court, [and] how to best behave in order to achieve a maximum outcome. [Joryn's] examples of poor and inappropriate behavior and conduct, resulting in bad outcomes, were poignant. As a fellow experienced family law collaborative and cooperative lawyer, I was especially pleased with [her] descriptions and comments about how the collaborative law process works. [Her] passion and zeal in helping clients navigate the divorce process out of the risky, expensive, public and enhanced ill-will which emanates from litigation, is clearly articulated....

"With this book, Joryn has "advanced and elevated the practice of collaborative law, showing how [the courtless option] is the best choice for those persons who wish a non-combative divorce process."

> **- Sheldon E. Finman, Collaborative Lawyer, Member, *Collaborative Family Law Council of Florida***

"Sadly, I met Joryn years after my 'War Story' divorce. Had I known Joryn then, perhaps my children would have suffered less. Perhaps I would not have had to move out of town, away from my kids, and to put thousands of miles on my vehicle for weekend visitation. Perhaps I would have been there for their games and school functions. Defaulting to traditional courtroom divorce is an all-too-frequent story. But it doesn't have to be that way. Anyone considering divorce should read this book. With Joryn as the voice of the Collaborative Process, the peace of collaborative divorce should be our future."

- **Gary Teaney, Father, CEO,** *Transformational Consulting for Business*

"My courtroom divorce was initiated by a trial lawyer who failed to explain my options before we filed. Thus began eight years of destructive litigation, primarily because my father-in-law was a trial attorney, *and* a retired Army general. By the time Joryn got involved, it was too late. As Joryn explains in *War or Peace*, it was 'war from the get-go.' Although I 'won' at trial, I still suffered through years of hearings, appeals, and post-divorce motions, and incurred attorney's fees I'm still paying off.

"I wish this book had been available back then; I would have known to ask about collaborative divorce. I might have avoided the sometimes overwhelming stress and the huge financial burden of constant litigation. This book explains how everyone benefits from avoiding the traditional courtroom process of divorce. Although Joryn was always able to see the bigger picture and kept me on task, sharing parent responsibility in the best interests of our child, it was not easy in the face of the endless litigation. No one really 'wins' in court."

- **Beth Hollis, Mother, Flight Attendant, Cancer Survivor**

"Divorce feels like an anchor, threatening to drag you to the bottom of the sea. I was blessed to be offered alternatives to the traditional courtroom divorce. In this book, Joryn shares with everyone the courtless alternatives she explained to me so many years ago. Joryn took care of my parting from my husband of so many years with gentle conversations between us; she led us through diligent discussions to an amicable conclusion that we could both live with. She morphed my anchor into a sail so that we could both move on. Now, as a result of those diplomatic discussions, we are still friends, fifteen years later. And we had no children together! I can only hope that others will benefit from Joryn's guidance as I have done."

- Jan Powell, Former Wife, Writer, Editor

"I never wanted a divorce, but there came a time when it was inevitable. So I sought out an attorney who appreciated that I didn't want a war; I wanted to ensure that my son would still have a relationship with both of his parents after our divorce. In her book, *War or Peace*, Joryn explains what she shared with me, that *how* we divorce is a choice. Granted we both had to choose the same option or we'd end up in court, but at least we knew there *was* a choice. Once Joryn armed me with that information, she made it possible for me to sit down with my husband and arm him, as well. It was because of her schooling that we were able to get through the stress and pain of terminating our marriage without spending every penny we had on legal fees. Reading this book will do the same thing for you, if you, too, are bound for divorce."

- Charmaine Disimile, Mother, Administrative Assistant

"Don't trust just any lawyer to tell you the best way to get divorced. Trust Joryn; read her book. She makes sense!"

- Sam Sorbo, Author, Nationally Syndicated Radio Talk Show Host

Table of Contents

Foreword

The title of this book, *War or Peace*, appropriately chosen by Joryn Jenkins, is an accurate description of the choice that is available when deciding to divorce.

There wasn't always such a choice; using litigating lawyers and the court system was the normal way to divorce – a way that leads almost always to acrimony and battle.

In 1989, as a trial lawyer, I became burned out from engaging in such battles, and was seriously considering giving up the practice of law. One day, in a moment of clarity, I saw that my job as a lawyer was to help my client (and to some extent the other client) achieve a reasonable settlement. I further saw that if settlement could not be achieved, the attorneys, as settlement lawyers, needed to withdraw from the case. So on January 1, 1990, I declared myself a collaborative (settlement) lawyer.

The idea took hold and today provides peaceful divorce settlement possibilities in 24 countries, with approximately 40,000 trained collaborative practitioners!

The concept of collaborative divorce is founded on positive, constructive principles such as love, sharing, communication, brainstorming, negotiation, and problem solving, and is meant to produce a mutually beneficial result. This is in stark contrast to the consequences that traditional courtroom divorce produces: depression, frustration, loathing, deceit, and mutually assured destruction.

The purpose of collaborative practice is to first and foremost take the judge out of the decision-making process. In what circumstance would you ever want a third party with whom you have no relationship, who doesn't know you or your kids, or share your values, to decide what will likely be the most critical decisions of your life?

Another objective of the collaborative process is to work only with attorneys who support settlement and who do not make acrimonious positional attacks.

Collaborative practice is also founded on the additional goal of maintaining some level of positive relationship with your soon-to-be ex-spouse. If you have children, this becomes even more vital.

And there is the related issue of maintaining the many relationships that surrounded and complemented your marriage: relationships with friends, with your spouse's family, with your neighbors, with your kids' teachers, and with all the others whose lives will be impacted, even if only indirectly, by your divorce.

The final objective of the collaborative approach is to save time and money.

When determining what method you should choose in charting your divorce, you could not have a better mentor than Joryn Jenkins and this book, *War or Peace*. She has worked in the legal profession as an attorney for 34 years. She has published extensively and served as editor-in-chief of three different legal publications. She spent two years as a full-time professor of law before returning to her first love: *practicing law so that she can make a difference in people's lives.*

Joryn is open-minded and has an evolutionary stance on "The Law," as it is always in flux and never static. This gives her a unique perspective, unlike those who are grounded in their traditional and sometimes archaic beliefs, such as courtroom divorce.

In *War or Peace*, Joryn is here every step of the way to guide you through the divorce process choices. And she does it methodically, with humor, and with true stories that illustrate her commentaries, recounting the events as she has witnessed them unfold, both those divorce wars that she herself has fought in the courtroom, as well as those peaceful divorces that she has helped negotiate in the conference room.

The choice is yours.

                         Stu Webb
                         Founder of Collaborative Law

CHAPTER ONE
Choose Your Fate:
Seven Courtless Divorce Options

In every jurisdiction in the United States, divorce must be recognized by a court by virtue of a "final judgment" of some kind in order to be effective. So when I say "courtless," I mean exactly that; these are processes that involve *less* court, rather than more. There is no such thing as a "no-court" option. The only question to be determined is which path a couple should take to obtain that final judgment dissolving their marriage to one another.

Divorce proceedings are often wrought with emotion and angst. Couples who decide to end their marriages have choices as to which divorce process they utilize. Too often, couples are simply unaware of their many alternatives. If divorce is in your future, you should understand the options so that you can employ the process that will work best for you and your family.

Most importantly: while legal action *is* required, litigation is *not*. And sometimes the road less taken is the better one. Just ask Robert Frost.

1) Default. This is the easiest divorce possible from most standpoints, but it is rarely likely. It involves no communication between the spouses and no negotiations whatsoever. In this situation, the spouses have usually already separated. One person wants the divorce; the spouse either does also or doesn't care, and has often disappeared. The first person files a divorce petition or complaint (depending on the jurisdiction) with the local judiciary and the spouse doesn't respond. The first person then asks the court to enter a default judgment (recognizing that the spouse "defaulted" by failing to answer the petition) and to grant the divorce requested.

2) Do-It-Yourself. We lawyers refer to this option as the *Kitchen Table Divorce.* You may choose to handle the dissolution of your marriage yourself, without hiring attorneys. If you haven't been married long, do not have children, and have few assets and liabilities, negotiating an agreement with your spouse and filing it in court on your own is not terribly difficult, will be the least expensive way to dissolve your marriage, and is the option most folks often choose. Many jurisdictions provide the necessary forms on their court websites. The forms contain specific instructions that are intended to be user-friendly. If you and your soon-to-be-ex are able to complete the forms, your only expense will be the filing fee. And then, in most jurisdictions, one of you must attend a court hearing to obtain the judge's execution of the final judgment of dissolution of marriage approving your marital settlement agreement.

Keep in mind, however, that even in the simplest divorce it is a good idea to have an attorney review your agreement before you file it. This brings us to *Courtless Option #3*.

3) *Kitchen-Table Plus*. Sometimes the spouses are able to reach an agreement together without the help of any professionals, but it's too complicated to use a simple form. Sometimes, they believe that they have reached an agreement, but one or both of them want an attorney's advice before signing anything. Whatever the reason, after the sit-down at the kitchen table, one of them then retains a lawyer who drafts what his client understands to be their settlement agreement. It is often beneficial to hire an attorney even if you and your spouse have reached an agreement in order to have legal eyes review it to let you know if you have left out any important issues.

However, the parties must understand that only one of them hired the attorney, and that the lawyer represents only *that* spouse's interests. Of course, the other spouse may also retain counsel to review the agreement prepared by the first and to advise him or her of its potential impact on their lives. If the lawyer advises his client that there are provisions that should be added or changed, then *Courtless Option #4* may result.

4) *One-Lawyer/One-Spouse Negotiations*. Sometimes one spouse hires an attorney before reaching an agreement with the first, but the other does not. Or the lawyer retained by one to review the agreement the couple thought they had reached advises his client that he recommends certain changes. The attorney then negotiates an agreement between the two spouses.

Again, the couple must be mindful that the attorney only represents the interests of the party who retained him or her. Assuming that the lawyer and the spouse who is unrepresented (called "*pro se*") ultimately reach a settlement agreement, again, the other spouse may then retain counsel to review the agreement prepared by the first and to advise him or her of its potential effects. This may result in *Courtless Option #5.*

5) Two-Lawyer/Two-Spouse Negotiations. This alternative is frequently called *Cooperative Divorce.* Sometimes both spouses retain lawyers to represent them in negotiating the terms of their divorce; sometimes they've already completed their kitchen table negotiations but, having both obtained the advice of counsel, have reopened those negotiations. Cooperative divorce is a principles-based dispute resolution process in which both spouses are represented by attorneys. It is settlement-focused, but leaves open the possibility of litigation if, and only if, it is absolutely necessary.

This process utilizes a framework for settlement which, if there are children of the marriage, promotes cooperative co-parenting later. If not, it simply supports the spouses' efforts to keep their divorce respectful and friendly, for the sake of their families, their mutual friends, and their own senses of self-worth. It reassures clients that their attorneys will try to settle the case. Assuming that both of the lawyers who are retained respect each other and can work well together, it minimizes inefficiency and unnecessary costs[1] while fostering civility and respect between the parties.

If the spouses hit a wall in their negotiations in any of the foregoing scenarios, *Courtless Option #6* is the next logical alternative.

6) Mediation. Mediation is a dispute resolution process in which an impartial person (the "mediator") facilitates settlement negotiations between the two spouses. The mediator may be an

---

[1] For a table comparing the cost of a typical collaborative divorce with the expense of a typical traditional courtroom divorce, go to the author's website at www.OpenPalmLaw.com.

3

attorney, a licensed mental health counselor, a certified public accountant, or some other specially-trained professional. The critical elements are that she is trained to mediate and to remain neutral; she does not represent either spouse. When considering which type of mediator to retain, you should consider the primary issues of your divorce. If you have children or a mentally ill spouse, for example, a counselor may be best because she is better trained to understand the developmental stages of children and how to most effectively negotiate with an ill person. If your issues are primarily financial, you may wish to hire a financial professional of some kind.

Mediation can be used in any of the alternative situations discussed above, except for *Default Divorce*. In mediation, the couple, either together or separately, either with counsel or without, sits with the mediator to work out their agreement. If the relationship has become oppositional, then the mediator will often work with both spouses at the same time, albeit shuttling back and forth between them in their separate rooms.

Mediation is intended to be interest-based, rather than positional. However, if the parties were not able to achieve their marital settlement agreement through any of the first four negotiation processes described above, it is likely because they are not able to back down from their "positions," and to identify their "interests" without the help of a very talented mediator.

In any event, an attorney will best understand the legal ramifications of your agreement, and even if you retain a counselor or financial professional to mediate the details of your divorce between just you two, you may still want to engage a lawyer to review your settlement agreement before it becomes official.

7) *Collaborative Process.* Collaborative practice ("CP") is a negotiation process that also occurs outside of court, but is specifically structured to ensure respectful and efficient meetings between the two spouses. The focus and objective of collaborative practice is to produce solutions that meet both participants' needs, and those of their children, if any, within a safe and confidential setting.

Most divorce processes address only the legal and financial separation between the parties. Many times the spouses have already taken care of the emotional element of the dissolution of their marriage. If not, however, the collaborative process enables a couple to end their marriage legally, financially, *and* emotionally— without sacrificing those relationships that they value most, as so often happens in court.

CP is based on three primary principles: the spouses' pledge not to go to court (i.e. to war); their pledge to an open and transparent, but private and confidential exchange of information; and solutions customized by the clients to account for the highest priorities of the adults, their children, and any other interested persons.

In CP, the clients each retain a lawyer, as well as a team of other professionals who are neutral — at least one mental health professional, usually a financial professional, and sometimes a child specialist. All CP team members, including the participants' lawyers, should be specially-trained in the collaborative paradigm, although a team may agree to the participants' choice of a professional who has not yet been trained collaboratively, if they believe that they can collaborate with the clients' nominee and that he will contribute to a successful outcome.

CP consists of a series of meetings: between each spouse and each neutral professional, between each spouse and his or her attorney, sometimes between both spouses and each neutral professional, and almost always of the full team, referring to all of the professionals, neutrals, lawyers, and both spouses. These meetings are intended to be non-confrontational, and to focus on the shared primary goal of finding an acceptable resolution between the spouses. Like the neutral team members, collaborative lawyers are trained to work with one another and the clients to manage communications, to ensure that each client is heard, and to explore each issue and possible solution fully. CP does not rely on court-imposed resolutions but instead permits the participants to negotiate in a safe and structured atmosphere of honesty, cooperation, integrity, and professionalism geared toward the future well-being of the restructured family.

The critical element of the collaborative process that

distinguishes it from any other is that the collaborative attorneys will withdraw and the spouses must retain separate trial attorneys if any adversarial proceedings ensue. This assures that everyone involved in the process is committed solely to the collaboration and its goals; no one splits his or her attention between collaborating and preparing for possible litigation in the event that the CP is terminated.

While participants may be more comfortable with the idea that they will not lose their attorneys if they cannot reach a settlement, the fact that the parties in *Divorce Options ##2-5* can easily choose litigation over settlement means that reaching a settlement is less likely than in the collaborative model.

Furthermore, while there are many ethical lawyers out there, many of them simply do not understand that we all have a conflict with our clients; we want to make money and our clients want to save money. CP eradicates most of this conflict by eliminating the lawyer's ability to "stir the pot," whether by design or by accident. The lawyer's sole job in the collaborative model is to help the clients satisfy their interests and settle their divorce. If he fails in that task and the collaboration terminates, then he loses his job. The parties then proceed to *Divorce Option #8*.

8) *Traditional Courtroom Divorce.* This is also known as litigation. In spite of the plethora of courtless divorce choices, the traditional divorce method is litigation, primarily because most couples are unaware of the choice that they could make if they wished to exercise that prerogative.

It is true that, with the advent of the internet, folks are becoming more educated about their options. Regardless, while the vast majority of litigating parties end up settling, many issues are still tried in the courtroom; settlements only come after interminable courtroom battles on which countless dollars are spent and endless time wasted. Rather than trying to settle matters amicably, attorneys file motions for even the simplest of issues. Parties play "discovery" games, refusing to provide financial documents so that the other side has to chase them down. The process tends to be expensive and hostile. It can destroy families who are already emotionally taxed and at odds with one another. And it fails to account for the fact that, in family law, once the divorce is finalized, the parties still have to deal with one another if children are involved.

The very few studies that have been conducted that compare the collaborative divorce model with the traditional courtroom divorce demonstrate that CP: 1) costs less; 2) takes less time; 3) is private and confidential; 4) causes less stress; 5) preserves relationships; and 6) produces customized results by which the former spouses are more likely to abide going forward.[2]

Couples who are able to negotiate their own dissolution of marriage agreements, rather than asking a judge to decide the details of their separation and their post-divorce lives, are more likely to abide by their settlement agreements. They suffer less post-divorce litigation because they "own" their agreements, decisions they have made for themselves.

Further, judges are limited at to what they can rule, and parties agreeing with each other have more leeway to formulate creative contracts that are more likely to fit their specific and sometimes unique needs.

Divorce discussions usually first focus on agreeing how those negotiations should occur. Understanding the different process options is an important first step in resolving your divorce as quickly, inexpensively, and as free of stress as possible.

---

[2] See the table comparing litigation and collaboration on page 148.

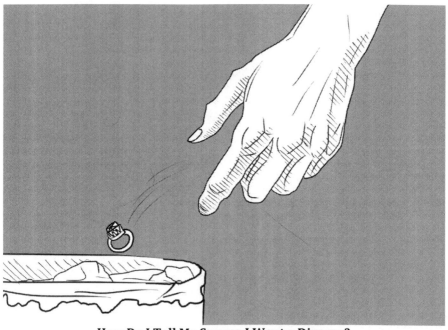

How Do I Tell My Spouse I Want a Divorce?

I have a lot in common with my clients. It helps me to empathize with their interests and concerns.

The Divorce

When I was 30, I finally got married. I was an assistant state attorney back then, and I loved my job. Consequently, I worked a lot, and didn't get out much, so the only people I knew socially were lawyers and cops. When I finally tied the knot, it was to another lawyer who had wooed me incessantly for seven months. I was not in a rush (I had never wanted children), but I *was* about to turn 30 years old. The way I saw it, it was time for me to get married, and he was a lawyer. I figured we had a lot in common.

When I say "he wooed me," by the way, I mean that I would have called it "stalking," had it happened today, 27 years later. I used to drive across the toll road in the mornings coming in to the office from the suburbs, and he would be waiting in his little burnt orange Corvette on the other side of the tollbooths. He would then follow me to the office, park near me (his office was in the same building), and invite me to breakfast. I never said "yes" (I'm not a breakfast person), although we often would then arrange to have lunch.

Soon, he started to write me poetry. It was not very good poetry, but that wasn't the point, was it? Clearly, he loved me.

I moved in with him.

Almost immediately, he proposed. It all seemed very romantic at the time. But once I agreed to marry him, he couldn't seem to wait. He pestered me to decide when. We tentatively set a date, but I kept changing it, putting him off.

I didn't know why then, although I do now.

Even after we set the date and made the arrangements, the day before the wedding, I tried to talk to my mother about my "cold feet." I really wanted permission to back out! She blew me off, told me that it was just because she had been married and divorced twice, that I was so anxious.

But that wasn't it.

Ultimately, we married on Valentine's Day, in a ceremony performed at a lovely restaurant, surrounded by 28 of our closest friends and family. (My fiancé wanted the wedding to be fairly informal.) In retrospect, most of these were MY friends, not his. Both of my best friends from high school had relocated to California, but they flew in, one from LA and the other from San Diego. All three of my sisters and my mother also attended, from four different states. I was the first of us girls to get married, and I was also the oldest.

Neither his brother nor his parents, all of whom lived in town, attended.

By that time, perhaps because he and I were already living together, the wedding was an anticlimax. I didn't want to take time off from my job as a prosecutor for a honeymoon, so, after the reception, we went back home. No big deal.

However, my husband changed his colors dramatically after that. Instead of returning home from work to a sweaty boyfriend who had just run 10 miles, I would invariably find my new husband propped up on the sofa, with the TV on. He gained 80 pounds in six months.

When I questioned him about it, he went to the doctor to discuss hypothyroidism. The doctor prescribed levothyroxin, one-a-day, but Charles would finish his monthly prescription in a week, trying to lose the weight faster, I suppose.

I remonstrated with him about the dangers of self-medicating, to no avail.

Soon after the wedding, he asked me to start paying the mortgage. He clarified that he could not, that his law business had slowed while he was busy romancing me, and that his firm was not bringing in enough to pay the overhead plus his salary. The house on Geneva Avenue was his (premarital), but he assured me, "I'm putting the deed in both of our names. After all, we're married now," he declared. "And it's only a temporary set-back."

I agreed to pay the $1600-a-month mortgage, which doesn't seem like much today, but it was exorbitant back then; it was all of my paycheck, after taxes. But the Geneva house was on Davis Islands, in one of the most genteel neighborhoods in Tampa.

It was around this time that I found a roll of hundred dollar bills in my husband's suit jacket pocket, a total of $5000. When I asked him about it, he shrugged, and said "It's a retainer. I didn't

10

get a chance to swing by the bank to deposit it. I'll do it tomorrow."

We'd been married for about a year when I started to notice money missing from my wallet. It's not a thing of which one can be sure; how often do you know *exactly* how much cash you're carrying? At least not back then, when we used cash far more often than we do today. However, it was dramatically brought home to me one specific day. I'll never forget it. I had gone to the bank to withdraw funds for groceries (this was before we could use credit cards at the grocery store), and I stopped home to compile my shopping list. Charles was home, watching TV. It didn't take me long to ponder the contents of our fridge and our cupboards and to itemize what we needed. I left soon after for Publix Supermarket, yelling "good-bye" as I ran out the front door.

Once there, I paced the aisles, working my way from one side of the store to the other, methodically loading my shopping cart with groceries and cleaning supplies. The bakery was my last stop, and then I headed for the register. My favorite cashier was on duty, and we chatted while she tallied up what I owed. "$126.35," Yvette announced.

I pulled out my wallet to retrieve seven $20 bills; I had withdrawn $200 from the bank. But all I had in my wallet was a single 20. "Whoops! I must've forgotten to get cash. I'll have to run to the bank," I explained. No bank machines back then. "Can you put my groceries in the cooler until I get back?"

I had "lost" $180 between withdrawing the money at the bank and arriving at Publix. My only stop had been at home. I had not left my wallet anywhere since leaving the house.

This occurred twice again in the next two months. I finally confronted Charles and demanded "what is going on?" He shrugged, and responded "I needed some money. It's no big deal." It was as simple and as inconsequential as that. At least for him.

I was upset, but nothing I said seemed to make a difference. He couldn't get it through his head that he should ask before taking. I would never have said "no," but I would have been able to plan for a little less embarrassment during my shopping expeditions.

One morning, upon my return from court, my secretary timidly approached me. She was apologetic, but protested that

Charles had stopped in shortly after I had left to ask her to do something that she could not do. Because she was uncomfortable saying "no" to him, she wanted me to take care of it. Perplexed, I asked her to explain.

"He asked me to notarize his client's signature without seeing him sign the documents and without verifying his driver's license." She continued, "He said his secretary was out today, or he'd have had her do it."

"Well, that's odd," I thought. Aloud, I inquired, "Did you ask him to have his client stop by to see you?"

"Of course, I did," she responded, piqued. "I explained the notary rules to him. I'm not an idiot." Nina never got irritated, but now she was annoyed, and not by me. "He told me he didn't want to bother the guy to come back just for that." She continued, "But it's against the rules for me to notarize someone's signature without verifying it."

I crossed the common hallway between my office and Charles' law firm, and grasped the handle to his front door. Before I could push it open, it opened before me, pulling me with it. Charles barreled into me. He stopped short and smiled, charmingly. "I was just coming to get you for lunch."

"Charles, Nina can't notarize someone's signature without verifying it. She needs to see your client, to inspect his driver's license, and to confirm that he signed the document you gave her."

"Not a problem." He was nonchalant. "She should have said so."

Well, now, that was odd; I *knew* she had.

The last straw came when Charles announced that he had sold our home. "What?" I was taken aback. "How could you sell it without my knowing? I thought you put my name on the title?" Silly me. It had never occurred to me to double check on that with the Recorder of Deeds.

"Well, I forgot to do that." Again, with the nonchalance. "Anyway, you have to sign off on the sale regardless. You're my wife." As if that fixed everything.

I seized the opportunity. I was just like anyone else; I didn't know how to tell my husband I wanted a divorce. Instead, I told him that I was upset that he had sold the house for which I'd been

12

paying for two years, and that I would sign off on the sale but that I wanted a separation to think things over.

What could he do? He acquiesced.

When I asked for the spare keys to my VW bug, he responded "Oh. I lost them." I believed him. Silly me.

I bought a small house not far from downtown; he rented an apartment somewhere on Davis Islands. I didn't ask exactly where.

Soon after our home sold, maybe a few weeks later, I noticed once again that money was missing from my wallet. I considered everyone with access to my office at the small boutique law firm for which I now worked. It just didn't seem possible.

But I couldn't even be sure that money was lost, not without paying closer attention to my spending habits. So I did. Sure enough, it happened again. This time, it was pretty clear that the cash was disappearing while I was at the gym, leaving my wallet in the briefcase in my car when I worked out every morning at 6 a.m.

It didn't immediately occur to me that Charles was taking it; after all, we didn't live together anymore.

The third time it happened, it struck me that Charles had not *lost* my car keys, he had simply kept them, planning ahead. He knew my habits, knew when I would be working out and where. And that I stashed my wallet in my briefcase back in those days, before I started carrying a purse.

That night, I was sitting in my new home, pondering what to do about the thefts. Dusk was just beginning to settle, and the crickets were just commencing their evening concert, which I quite liked, when I heard a peculiar noise outside, a twig breaking? A sound that didn't belong. I peeked out one of the windows, peering between the blinds, rather than lifting them. And there was Charles, off to the right, skulking in the bushes that surrounded and protected my small domain, trying unsuccessfully to stare through the window next to mine.

I ran to the phone. I called his apartment. It rang four times. Then the answering machine picked up, as I knew it would. "Charles, I want a divorce. I'll have Raphe take care of it."

Raphe was the guy in my new workplace who practiced family law. The next morning, I stopped by his office. He was already at his desk, thank goodness. "I need to get divorced," I announced, without introduction.

He looked up, appraisingly. I'm sure he was wondering what had brought that on, but he didn't ask me any questions. Not then. I'm sure he didn't want to intrude on my privacy, and firm policy assured me free legal services by a fellow lawyer, if he did that kind of work. Which Raphe did. "Not a problem. Fill out an intake form." (To his secretary, just outside the door, he barked "Sharon, get a dissolution of marriage intake form for Joryn." Then he continued.) "I'll get the petition filed right away. Then we can discuss logistics."

My heart leapt into my throat. "What?!" I raised my voice, in shock. Before I could stop myself, I blurted "You have to file a lawsuit to get divorced? I have to sue him to get divorced? I have to go to court to get divorced?" Raphe smiled (at my naiveté, I suppose). But I continued "I didn't have to go to court to get married! I have to go to court to get divorced?!"

I had been practicing law for nine years. But I didn't know that you have to go to court to obtain a final judgment of divorce. I had no reason to know; divorce was not in my wheelhouse. And it was not so common as it is now that most people are aware that you go to court to get divorced. In fact, now we assume we must go to court, when we really don't. And that's what the lawyers don't tell us now.

Eventually, after he explained the process (remember, this was 25 years ago, before mediation was standard practice), I explained to Raphe that I wanted nothing except what I had brought into the marriage two years earlier. He prepared a settlement agreement and proffered it to Charles, who executed it and returned it the same day.

I was very lucky.

I was married on Valentine's Day; I was divorced on Halloween. My secretary, who scheduled the final hearing, thought it appropriate.

14

I've learned a lot in this business. My clients have taught me a great deal about insecurity and self-confidence, passion and addiction, pride and sympathy. One thing I now know for sure; things are rarely as they first appear.

As a result, I've discovered that it is critical to help people feel at ease during their initial consultations so that they feel comfortable enough to divulge their very private personal interests and concerns. My ability to share my own stories, my own failures and faults, if you will, has stood me in good stead. It makes it easier for my clients to share in their turn.

But it is my ability to remain open to understanding and appreciating lives very unlike my own, to empathize with my clients, that has led me to some of my most interesting cases, including the following. Although this began as a traditional courtroom divorce, it ended up being courtless, in part because I insisted on early and open exchange of our financial information and mediation, but also because my client was so savvy to the positional bargaining in which her wife insisted on engaging.

The Transformed

Paul first contacted me by phone with a very ordinary-sounding divorce. Well, as ordinary as they ever are, at least. He had been sent to me by a lady lawyer I knew, and liked. She had referred him because she (and he) was uncomfortable continuing to represent him. This information raised my antennae. What was going on here? I asked him for more details.

He was a former Army Ranger, married for over sixteen years. Four hundred parachute jumps. In charge of the search for Osama Bin Laden for two years. They had no children, just two dogs that they adored. His wife wanted alimony, and there were assets to be distributed between them; they had accumulated real estate over the years as he had been reassigned to different commands. He also had property he had accrued before they were married. Oh, *and* he owned the largest privately-owned military history book collection in the world.

He was still a colonel in the army, but had been reassigned to Langley; she had stayed behind in Tampa and had recently filed for divorce.

Sounded perfectly normal.

Then Paul dropped the atom bomb. He divulged that he suffered from "gender dysphoria," a medical condition in which a person's anatomical sex at birth does not match his or her gender identity. He explained, "To put it simply, I feel like a woman stuck in a man's body."

I wanted Paul to feel comfortable, so I did my best to hide my surprise; I had never come across anyone suffering from Paul's condition. "How long have you felt this way?"

Paul responded quickly and passionately, "As long as I can remember. It has caused me severe psychological distress and intense feelings of discomfort. Since I was a baby, my sex was classified as male. Accordingly, my parents gave me the traditionally male name "Paul John," and, from a young age, I was socialized to wear traditionally masculine attire and to participate in traditionally masculine activities. Because of my severe discomfort, I gravitated towards highly masculine activities to prove that I was a man."

Fascinated, I replied, "So what made you realize that you no longer wanted to live this way?"

"I just could not continue to live a lie. As I got older, I wanted to feel comfortable in my own skin. Over time, I determined that the gender designation assigned to me at birth did not conform with my gender identity. I sought sex reassignment. Initially, I've begun living full-time as a woman. Eventually, I will undergo hormone therapy, and finally, sex-reassignment surgery."

I was a bit confused. He sounded like a guy. "How far into the process are you?"

"Actually, I have just begun to live as a woman. Please call me "Paula." I first approached you as "Paul" because I needed to gauge your reaction to my situation before I trusted you enough to retain you. That's why Mary referred me to you; she and I just couldn't connect, but she thought that you might be able to."

Wow. Talk about some heavy lifting. What could I do to empathize with . . . Paula? I explained that I had never had occasion to become familiar with "gender dysphoria" (she laughed, "Yeah, I get that!"), and I asked if there were any resources that might help me to understand how she felt.

Without hesitating, she directed me, "Read *She's Not There*. It's a great book by a professor in New Hampshire who suffers from gender dysphoria herself. Call me when you've finished reading it."

Amazon delivered the book to me within three days. It was a quick, discomfiting, but nevertheless enjoyable read. Paula retained me shortly thereafter. I was pleased that I had helped her feel comfortable enough to trust me with the restructuring of her life, even though she was still in the early stages of her sexual reassignment. Later, I realized that she had had to make a decision, and she was very, very good at that (she *was* a colonel, after all), despite the stress that the divorce (one of the most stressful events that anyone can suffer through) caused her, coupled with the strain that her sexual reassignment undoubtedly also generated.

Her three brothers, her father, and her mother were all incredibly supportive. Lucky gal!

Over time, I learned a lot about Paula. We became friends. I enjoyed her company, and found her true life stories fascinating. Paula enjoyed many traditionally female activities. We often gabbed about hair, makeup, and clothing. She described herself as a lesbian. (We joked that she was "a lesbian trapped in a man's body.") She explained that gender identity is different from sexual preference. Even though her gender had changed, her sexual preference remained the same.

Paula's wife was not interested in the collaborative divorce option. She was banking on the traditional courtroom divorce to coerce Paula into a settlement very favorable to her.

Naturally, we were (randomly) assigned a very old-fashioned judge. In court, I referred to Paula as "she," while her wife's attorney adamantly referred to her as "he," not wanting to recognize Paula's gender dysphoria. I must admit that it was difficult to say "Her wife would not..." without laughing. The obvious gender dissonance in such a statement caused aftershocks in my brain!

The judge was clearly confused as to which pronoun was appropriate!

For obvious reasons, I was especially leery of taking Paula's case to trial. Although her wife, a petite brunette with childlike eyes, had been well aware from the inception of the marriage of Paula's gender discomfort, she was now claiming it was news to her. Regardless of the truth of the matter, she was extremely angry and very vindictive. I focused Paula on settling the case, and we took it to mediation as soon as we were able.

This worked out well for Paula; by the time we convened in the mediator's offices, Paula was unemployed and, I argued, unlikely to find an occupation paying anything close to what she had made as a colonel. On the other hand, the parties had accumulated nine properties over time, some Paula had purchased before the marriage and some they had purchased together during it. (As she had been transferred from city to city, she had retained the homes she lived in and rented them out when she was relocated.) So although her wife had not worked outside the home for the last ten years, at 41, she was still relatively young, and we had real estate with which to negotiate.

Negotiations were not easy, but the most difficult interest to satisfy was Paula's fierce desire to retain her prize possession, her library. She owned the world's largest privately-owned military history collection, books accumulated over the twenty-five years of her career. Her wife took the position that it was half hers, a not unreasonable position to take when you anticipate asking a judge to make the decision; most of the books had been purchased during the marriage and were therefore, legally, "marital." The judge, therefore, of course, would just "split the baby." But her wife's real interest was in getting back at Paula somehow; I could envision her burning her half of the books were she to end up with them.

Because we were forced to negotiate from positions, rather than from interests, I retained a personal property valuation expert. So did my opposing counsel. This was the smartest course of action we could have taken, but only because we were lucky; the street value of the collection was *de minimus*, according to both experts. On my advice, Paula offered her wife a cash sum that far exceeded the value of half of the books, and so she was satisfied with her "pound of flesh."

Eventually, because we convinced Paula's wife that she was

unlikely to make the same kind of income going forward that she had made in the army, we were able to trade Paula's individually owned (premarital) property for her wife's alimony claim, and the case settled relatively quickly after that.

Once we were able to finalize Paula's divorce, she applied for a position as a Terrorism and International Crime Research Analyst with the Congressional Research Service of the Library of Congress. She was exceptionally well-qualified for this position, as a twenty-five year veteran of the U.S. Armed Services, and having served in a variety of critical command and staff positions, including those in Armored Cavalry, Airborne, Special Forces and Special Operations Units, and in combat operations such as those in Panama, Haiti, and Rwanda. Promoted to colonel, she had distinguished herself with numerous awards, decorations, and qualifications over the course of her career. She was a distinguished graduate of both the National War College and Army Command and General Staff College, and held master's degrees in history and international relations.

Approximately two months after submitting her application for the Terrorism Research Analyst position, Paula was invited to interview with three representatives of the Congressional Research Service. As she had not yet changed her legal name or begun presenting as a woman at work, she had submitted her application under her legal name and went to the interview dressed in traditionally masculine attire.

After the interview committee spoke to her references and reviewed her writing samples, Paula was informed that she had been selected for the position. And, after resolving issues over salary, Paula accepted it.

It was then that she explained to the interview committee that she was under a doctor's care for gender dysphoria and that, consistent with her doctor's instructions, she would be using a traditionally feminine name, dressing in traditionally feminine attire, and otherwise living and presenting herself full-time as a woman when she started work as the Terrorism Research Analyst. She even showed the committee photographs in which she was dressed in traditionally feminine workplace-appropriate attire.

Although nothing was said to suggest that this information

would impact the Library's hiring decision, the following day, Paula was notified that, after a "long, restless night," the committee had decided that, "for the good of the service," and "given Paula's circumstances," Paula would not be a "good fit" at the Library of Congress.

Paula was forced to file an administrative complaint with the Equal Employment Opportunity Office of the Library of Congress in which she alleged that the Library's decision to rescind its job offer because she is transgender constituted impermissible sex discrimination in violation of Title VII. While I did not represent her in that litigation, she often contacted me to obtain my advice, and ultimately obtained a judgment in her favor. By that time, however, having been one of the military's foremost anti-terrorism experts, and having also been highly successful in maintaining the many friendships she had accumulated during her military service (despite her transformation,) she was self-employed as an anti-terrorism consultant to the military, making well into the six-figures, and no longer in need of a job.

Avoiding the Destruction of a Courtroom Divorce

Everyone knows that a relationship that was not healthy to begin with is likely to result in divorce, or some other dissolution of that relationship. Dealing with the emotional repercussions of the official or legal termination of the relationship can be traumatic. Sometimes, the trauma can even turn deadly; we've all read about the judge or attorney or party who was shot after the hearing by the unhappy ex-spouse. Court-related deaths are more common in family law cases than in any other, including criminal law cases, where the defendant doesn't blame the court for his problems.

Arguably, blaming the system for break-up-related problems is not without justification, as this client's story aptly illustrates.

The Boyfriend

Dan Francesco, the arrogant son of a bone surgeon in our small town, entered our lives when I was fourteen. Even at sixteen, he projected a God complex. His pompous air of entitlement revealed the life of a kid who has never had to work that hard at anything.

Beneath his cocky exterior bubbled a palpable insecurity that fueled his aggression. Along with steroids. And watching his father beat his mother for years.

Though I hate to admit it, he was good-looking, the dark, brooding type. Behind his back, we called him the "Italian Stallion." His deep, penetrating eyes and pale skin implied intelligence that he, at least, thought was higher than it was. Even as a teen, he regularly tried to scam people and get something for nothing. He had a propensity for that.

Not tall, but large, he outsized his girlfriend, my petite ninety-five pound, 4'11" sister, Kelly.

Kelly and I were only two years apart and had always been close. Two peas in a pod, we both took after our athletic, cheerful, Lilliputian-sized parents. But Dan's negative view of life erased any optimistic outlook. His sulking demeanor made him too serious, overly sensitive to any joke at his expense, a misfit in my jovial little family. Clearly he disliked me and my parents, but we all did our best to keep up appearances, for Kelly's sake.

Folks in town rejected him as well. His reputation for cruelty and superciliousness limited his close friends to two. His best friend, Derek, displayed the slow traits resulting from fetal alcohol syndrome. But Derek was an extremely nice guy, forever loyal to Dan, but also a protector of Kelly. Dan liked him because Derek knew his place, far below Dan.

His only other true friend was Kelly.

He didn't care for me either. Though I felt the same, I hid it. I think he resented my scholastic and social achievements; he felt inferior. I unnerved him because I represented the independence that he feared Kelly might seek. He didn't want me to give her any ideas.

The story of one of Dan's other "friends" illustrates our cause for concern. Little Dickey Farr brutally slayed his ex-girlfriend's parents and then shot himself to death in 2003, after she broke up with him.

Dick and Amy were high school sweethearts and had continued to date for several years thereafter while attending the local college. Before killing himself, Farr called his parents and told them that he had killed his girlfriend's parents because she had "ignored his calls" and been "mean" to him. During the long hours of the standoff before his suicide, his ex-girlfriend spoke with detectives. He had always had a violent streak, had always been insecure and unstable. While they were still dating, he'd once slapped her across the face while we were all at a party. Even she didn't know why, although we all thought it might have been the harmless flirting she had engaged in with some visiting college kid.

Following their break-up, he had scared her by stalking her. Thus her ultimate crime of "ignoring" him and being "mean" to him. Amy has spent the last eleven years wondering what she might have done to prevent her parents' untimely deaths.

Amy and Dick's relationship was so similar to Kelly and Dan's that we all feared for Kelly's safety, and ours, if she ever summoned the courage to break up with him. But our fears for her safety began long before 2003.

Dan was the first guy Kelly had dated. They started going out when they were about sixteen. They began dating before Dan had ended his previous relationship. But who can stop young love? Looking back, I know that Kelly wishes she was that scorned girl, free to proceed with a happy young adulthood.

Dan's drinking began in high school. At first, he entertained others; he was "the life of the party." Inevitably, though, he would pick a fight with Kelly. Although she tried to shield us from his violent behavior, we lived in a small town; we knew. However, we didn't know the extent of it and passed it off as youthful passion.

One night in high school when my parents were out of town, I returned home from cheerleading practice and found Dan drunk and sobbing on our bathroom floor. My sister made excuses for the bruises on her face.

Another time, my parents had to call his father to come pick him up from our house because Dan was drunk and upset. This was only one of three occasions when the parents met, despite the fact that we all lived in the same small town. We assumed that they, like Dan, believed themselves better than us. Perhaps they did. Or perhaps they were afraid to know us better.

My mother wanted to put an end to their relationship. But my father believed that prohibiting contact would drive them closer together, like a couple of star-crossed lovers. Nobody thought they would stay together when they both went off to college.

Unfortunately, Kelly followed Dan to college in Gainesville. A couple years later, I went there, too. Though we lived in the same town again, Kelly and I barely had a relationship because of Dan's control over her. When we went home for holidays, she avoided us and spent most of her time with him.

I majored in psychology. I didn't know why at the time, but it seems obvious in retrospect. After graduation, they returned to our hometown. Years passed. He remained a louse with a horrendous temper. They lived together but never married. I didn't know why, but I didn't ask, afraid to open the door to the subject in case I was to plant the seed.

I hoped that the physical abuse would stop when he went off steroids and his hormones matured. However, the emotional abuse continued, and Kelly's personality faded. No longer a vibrant person, she was just "Dan's girlfriend."

Then he proposed; they were engaged for several years. Every time they'd start planning the wedding, she'd find a reason to wait. Thank God.

Thankfully, this isn't the tale of a battered woman killed by her abuser. Late one Saturday night, thirteen years into their relationship, she called me sobbing. By this time, I had graduated from law school and taken a job practicing law in a real city. She had called the police because Dan had beaten her. She hysterically explained, "We attended a concert earlier today, and he drank a lot. When we got home, he picked a fight with me. He chased me into our bedroom and held me down hard on our bed, and then slammed me against the walls. He held me down in the empty bathtub." Hearing her story, I was trying to be strong for her, but I was fighting back waves of nausea.

Bruises covered her body, the angry tattoos bearing witness to the violence she had suffered. Kelly pressed criminal charges against Dan and petitioned for a temporary restraining order. I tried to advise her, but, like a surgeon who should not operate on her own family, it was extremely difficult to provide her with sound legal advice.

I turned to my friends in the local bar association for help. Beyond the injunction and criminal charges, though they never wed, Dan and Kelly had been living as a married couple for years. Therefore, they had assets and liabilities to distribute. During their relationship, he controlled the finances...just another example of his control over her. She routinely wrote large checks from her personal account to him. They were building a home and he spent this money on the construction and on their living expenses. She didn't want the home, but we felt that she was entitled to a portion of nearly $115,000 that she had contributed. It was the one thing she could take away from the relationship.

At some point, Kelly quitclaimed the home they were building to Dan. She doesn't remember doing that and maintains that she'd never have willingly done so. It seemed clear he forged her name, defrauding her by taking money from her (presumably for investment) and then not putting her name on the investment.

When we contacted Dan's father to discuss how the families might be able to help Dan and Kelly reach a settlement, he responded as we expected. He refused to discuss it and accused Kelly of trying to extort funds from Dan.

Kelly attended the injunction hearing unrepresented and pled her own case. Dan was represented by counsel who echoed his father's accusation that Kelly was attempting to extort money from his son. Keep in mind that the injunction hearing occurred in the little town where we grew up. The judge, who likely ran in the same circles as Dan's surgeon father, would have known of Dan's aggressive reputation, especially toward Kelly.

How any judge could look at my tiny crying sister compared to big, intimidating Dan, see the pictures of her bruises from Dan's attack on her, and conclude anything other than that she was the epitome of a battered woman I do not know. At first, Dan's attorney swayed him until my sister and mother broke down completely, and the judge granted the injunction.

Dan retaliated. He filed a completely frivolous and vexatious complaint for damages against Kelly, my parents, *and* me, claiming that Kelly was attempting to extort funds from him. Who was the extorter now?

By this time, my tiny family was stressed and scared. Experience shows that litigation expenses can quickly skyrocket and that the person with the deeper pockets (Dan) is usually the one who eventually wins, one way or another. I was well aware of this. I had no doubt that Dan and his family would pursue this ridiculous case to continue bullying Kelly. No one in our family could handle the idea of this litigation being dragged out, especially considering Kelly's frailty after the emotional beating she'd suffered. So, when Dan offered that we pay him $20,000 and agree to dismiss the injunction in return for his dismissal of his baseless complaint, we agreed. I would never have advised a client to accept such an absurd offer, but my family's only priority was Kelly's emotional health, and putting a quick end to our relationship with Dan was really the only option for us. If we had not accepted the offer, I can only imagine the horrifying war that would have ensued.

At the hearing to dismiss the injunction, the judge asked Kelly to explain why she wanted to let it go. Continuing seemed pointless because Dan was still stalking her, demanding that it be dismissed to settle other litigation. Kelly stared at her hands, clasped tightly together atop the podium, at the fingers on her left hand massaging the fingers on her right, and then vice versa, in an endless attempt to relieve her anxiety. The judge didn't pressure her to answer. Instead, he agreed to her request.

Dan continued to stalk Kelly. She quickly began dating a much older gentleman, and soon they wed. We worried that it was too soon and that she was too fragile to make such a huge life decision. I think that she believed it was the only way to be safe. Her husband moved her thousands of miles away and built her a home in the middle of nowhere. Although she still has nightmares about Dan, we are at peace knowing that he no longer dominates her life.

Someone Always Loses in Court; Sometimes Both Do!

CHAPTER TWO
Top Tips for Getting Divorced

When will the stress stop? When will the confusion go away? When will my life be normal again? And, by the way, what *is* the new normal?

Divorce is frightening. There are so many questions. Here are just the most obvious:

1. How do I do it?
2. How do I tell my spouse?
3. What will happen to the kids?
4. Will I have to move out of my home?
5. Will all my personal information become public?
6. How long will it take?
7. How much will it cost?
8. Do I have to have a lawyer?
9. Do I have to go to court?

If we believe that the best of all possible worlds is that nothing will change – that everything is perfect just as it is, we will be very disappointed. Change is the only constant – kids grow up, friends grow old, our health declines, people die, our memories fade – life is one big change – and we are always in a state of transition – adapting to the current reality. The craziness of change might be coming from your resistance to this fact of life!

And divorce is change, let there be no doubt. It is a well-known fact that divorce is one of the biggest stresses one can suffer in a lifetime; and this death of a long-term relationship, your marriage, is often compounded by another big stressor, moving out of your home.

So here are my best tips to help you deal with the stress of the change that is divorce.

Accept what is. As you look around and you see everything as it shouldn't be, the resistance to what is can drain your energy and deplete your reserves. It is. And you can't do much about what has happened. You can, however, have a significant impact on how you react to what is, and you can also have a significant impact on what will happen in the next minute, hour, day, month, and year if you turn your attention towards what you want instead of what you don't want. Visualize your future after divorce. This is a fresh start, a new beginning. It's an exciting time, not a depressing time. You can make it happen by envisioning it. Mantras *do* work.

Attend to what you say. Every time you hear yourself talking about what you don't want, realize that you are attracting more of what you don't want to you! Want to attract more good stuff? Then talk about good stuff and what you are doing to move in the direction of the good stuff. Talk about the wonderful life you will be living after your divorce is finalized.

That being said, you must also appreciate when to be quiet and listen. If you are able to hear your spouse's point-of-view, you will likely be more willing to consider possible settlements.

Focus on your future. Talk with others about what you want. Not as in "what I want for me," but as in what you want for everyone who is important to you – your family, your community, your gender, your profession, and your world. Then listen and be willing to accept what they offer. Sure, you can do it alone, but why struggle? Why not graciously accept the gifts that others offer to you? Besides, it's more fun, isn't it?

What does the world around you look like in this Utopian life after divorce? How are the kids doing in school and in life? How is your ex moving on? How wonderful is your job, now that you are able to focus and to achieve in it? What fabulous gifts are you now able to give back to the world?

Choose your divorce process. Understand that there are multiple divorce processes, and you are not required to litigate. Instead, you could mediate or negotiate your divorce collaboratively. Be sure to speak with an attorney who understands these different courtless options. And, before you hire an attorney, get a second opinion.

Focus on interests, rather than on positions. Identify your interests, and understand that there may be several ways to achieve your goals. This will give you more bargaining room and increase the likelihood that both parties will accomplish their most important goals with fewer compromises. For example, if you and your spouse have one orange, and you each focus on your position that you want the whole orange, one of you will win the orange, and one of you will lose the orange, or you may cut the orange in half, and neither of you will be satisfied. However, if you focus on your separate interests in the orange, you may be able to come to a win-win solution. You may want the zest so that you can make a dessert. Your spouse may want the pulp to make juice. Understanding your interests will allow you to win the peel, and your spouse to win the pulp; you both win!

Be realistic! Even if you need alimony, that doesn't mean that your spouse has the ability to pay it. Even though you would like to stay in your home, that doesn't mean that it is financially possible for you to do so. Just because you want your children with you the vast majority of the time, it is not fair to your spouse to have less time with your children than you do if she wants the same. Divorcing spouses waste time and money arguing impossible positions. Try to see the big picture, and take time to view issues from your spouse's perspective. Consider what your interests are, and don't just take a position for the sake of taking a position.

Remember that your attorney is on your side. He has your best interests at heart. Just because he is telling you something that you do not want to hear, doesn't mean that he doesn't understand what you want. Do not treat your attorney as your enemy.

Understand that you have signed a contract with your attorney. If you don't understand the terms of it, ask your attorney questions. If you are not comfortable with the amount of time billed on your case, discuss it with your attorney sooner rather than later. Your attorney may have some less expensive options for his representation of you, and it is better to explore those options before you owe your attorney fees that you cannot afford. No one likes to spend a lot of money on an attorney, only to discover that the money is gone but the divorce is still plowing forward. And you're representing yourself without a clue how to do it.

Do your homework. Any divorce takes a lot of hard work. You will need to prepare a financial affidavit, compile financial documents, review lengthy settlement offers, attend a parenting course, prepare for hearings and depositions, etc. The more work you do, the more that you will be committed to resolving the matter, and the less you will have to pay your attorneys and other professionals to do the work for you or to chase you down to do the work they requested of you.

Be transparent. By freely disclosing information, you will gain your spouse's trust, and you will save money by avoiding the other side having to search for information. You are required by Florida law to disclose everything, and by doing so, you will develop the trust necessary to settle your divorce and to move forward with your ex as amicably as possible.

Observe the Golden Rule. Treat your spouse as you would like to be treated. Don't lie to, belittle, or ignore him or her. Don't empty joint bank accounts, dissipate marital assets, or remove your spouse from insurances. Don't file false police reports or contact child services unless your children really are in danger. Don't post inappropriate pictures and comments on social media.

Most importantly, understand that, if you have children, your divorce does not end your relationship with your spouse. You will have to deal with him or her daily until your children turn 18, and even thereafter, at major events like graduations and weddings. It is important to be as amicable as possible during your divorce so that you are able to be in the same room with one another in the future.

Do not speak disparagingly about each other to your children, friends, or family. Your spouse will hear about it, and it will only delay your ability to resolve your divorce and move on. Your spouse will be less likely to negotiate reasonably with you if you are constantly badmouthing him or her. While divorces are highly emotional times, try to remember that there is life after divorce, and you should avoid doing things during your divorce that are destructive to your relationships with your spouse and with his or her family, with your children, and with your friends and neighbors.

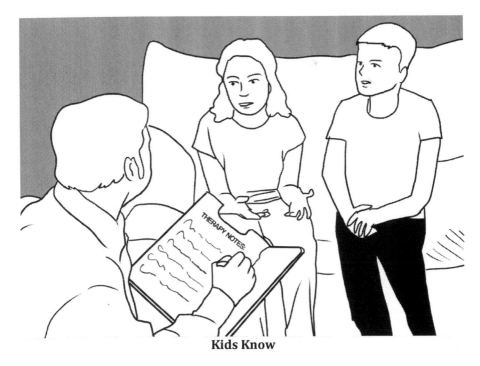

Kids Know

Trial work is very much about being prepared. When I was a law professor teaching Trial Practice, I mentioned in nearly every class that being prepared was the most critical aspect of trial work. Trial lawyers spend an extraordinary amount of time preparing for each and every evidentiary hearing at which we appear. Unless we've clued them in beforehand, our clients are often not prepared to pay what must seem to them to be the excessively high cost of going to trial. I learned when I was very young that preparation may take a lot of time, but it's critical, and may be life-changing.

Stupid

I do not recall much from before I was in second grade. I remember Becky and Laurie, the two little girls who lived next-door to us in La Jolla, who were the same ages as me and Mickey, my younger sister. I remember the blue plastic slip 'n' slide that we all had so much fun playing on the summer I was five and Mickey was two, and the matching quilts that Mickey and I had in the blue and green version, and Laurie and Becky had in the maroon and pink, on our two sets of matching twin beds.

I do not remember *ever* not being able to read.

When I was six years old, according to my mother, I "graduated" from first grade. My teacher waited until then to tell my mother that I was "stupid." She explained, as she handed my mother the cute little diploma that my public elementary school had mocked up for us, that she had even toyed with the idea of holding me back a year. It was only then that my 27-year-old mother, as she tells the story, discovered that I was still unable to read.

For some reason, my mother was offended by this and I paid the piper. I spent the entire summer between first and second grade, "in school." I was to study from 9:00 AM until at least noon every day, without exception, learning not only how to read, but also at least one year's worth of math before the end of the summer vacation. My mother began each morning by teaching me the new concepts and by reviewing the mechanics I had already learned. I was not released from "class" until I had read the specified chapters of a novel chosen by my mother and had completed (correctly) a certain number of pages from my math book. I had no sooner completed one math book or finished reading one work of fiction than my mother assigned me another.

I vividly recall sitting in my bedroom at my desk, which had been placed under the window looking out upon Galway Circle, which fronted our house. I spent my mornings that summer at that little writing table, occasionally staring out the window at all of the other little kids on my block playing together, while I was stuck inside, working math problems.

That was the summer that I read *Robinson Crusoe*. Initially, the massive volume was intimidating; my mother had bought me the fifth graders' version of the novel. So it seemed it would be quite the ordeal, but, halfway through it, after his shipwreck but before Friday appeared on the scene, I began to understand how it felt to be scared and alone in the world! I wanted to find out what would happen to poor Robinson Crusoe next!

My father did not believe me when I told him I had finished reading the book. He bet me a silver dollar that I could not convince him that I had read it thoroughly. So he sat down at the kitchen table, with his chair turned towards me, to listen to me tell him the story while my mother made dinner, and occasionally turned around to smile at the two of us. I stood between my father's knees and, I am certain, bored him to death by reciting every single detail of the voyager's lengthy saga. In fact, before I was halfway through, he put his hands up in surrender and congratulated me on doing a good job.

He gave me the silver dollar. I am now 57 years old. I still have the silver dollar.

So I did go into second grade, but without understanding that I had already learned everything Mrs. Seward was scheduled to teach me. I remember sitting in the back of the classroom, and being allowed to read whatever I wanted to read. (By then, I could "not get enough," as my mother proudly put it.)

My mother proceeded to try to convince the administration that I should be moved up into the third grade. For months, they would have none of it.

It was not until she threatened to teach me Latin, in February of that year, that they finally conceded. One of the teaching assistants showed up at my second grade classroom, had a whispered conversation with my teacher, beckoned me to accompany her, and helped me gather up my belongings. I had no idea what was going on, but I was accustomed to following instructions from adults and went with her. She took me across the courtyard to a third-grade classroom, walked me inside, introduced me to the teacher, and showed me to a seat that had apparently already been assigned to me, settling me there.

I soon discovered that I was two thirds of the year behind the rest of the class in learning to write cursive. Luckily for me, I was far ahead of the class in my ability to read (at the 5th grade level), and in math, so I spent all of my time trying to catch up in writing script. This involved staying after school every day for two months learning the first half of the alphabet, while, during the regular school day, I learned the second half with the rest of the class.

I made no friends that year. But I was never called "stupid" again.

Preparing for Divorce

CHAPTER THREE
The Seven Biggest Divorce Mistakes

MISTAKE #1
ASSUMING YOU MUST LITIGATE

There are various ways to dissolve your marriage that don't require contested litigation. While a judgment of divorce signed by a judge is required, there are diverse routes that lead to that final hearing. Not all paths to the courtroom lead *through* the courthouse. You can negotiate an agreement at your kitchen table. You can hire a mediator to help both of you work out the agreement. You can retain a cooperative lawyer to work it out with your spouse or with her cooperative lawyer. Or you can employ a collaborative team to help you both negotiate your divorce. If you are successful in one of these forms of alternative dispute resolution, you will be required to attend a brief final uncontested hearing so that the judge can enter your final judgment, but you will avoid scary hearings and intimidating depositions.

As discussed in more depth in Chapter One, you may choose to handle your divorce yourself, without hiring attorneys. If you haven't been married long, do not have children, and have few assets and liabilities, negotiating an agreement with your spouse and filing it in court on your own is not terribly difficult. It will be the least expensive way to dissolve your marriage, and is the option people often choose.

Some people are able to reach an agreement without the help of any professionals, but it's too complicated to use a simple form. Others believe that they have reached an agreement, but one or both of them want an attorney's advice before signing anything. Whatever the reason, after the sit-down at the kitchen table, one of them may then retain a lawyer who drafts what his client understands to be their settlement agreement.

At times, one spouse hires an attorney, but the other does not, and the attorney and the other spouse negotiate. Or the lawyer retained by one spouse to review the agreement the couple thought they had reached recommends certain changes. Again, the attorney then negotiates an agreement with the unrepresented spouse.

Another alternative is cooperative divorce, which is a principles-based dispute resolution process in which both parties are represented by attorneys. It is settlement-based, but leaves open the possibility of litigation if, and only if, it is absolutely necessary.

Mediation is a dispute resolution process in which an impartial person facilitates settlement negotiations between the two spouses. In mediation, the couple, either together or separately, either with counsel or without, sits with the mediator to work out their agreement. If the relationship has become oppositional, then the mediator will often work with both spouses at the same time, albeit shuttling back and forth between them in their separate rooms.

Collaborative practice is a negotiation process that also occurs outside of court, but is specifically structured to ensure respectful and efficient meetings between the two spouses. The focus and objective of collaborative practice is to produce solutions that meet each person's needs, and those of their children, if any, within a safe and confidential setting. This enables a couple to end their marriage legally, financially, *and* emotionally, without sacrificing those relationships that they value most, as so often happens in court.

CP is premised on three primary principles: the spouses' pledge not to go to court (i.e. to war); their pledge to an open and transparent, but private and confidential exchange of information; and solutions customized by the participants to account for the highest priorities of the adults, their children, and any other interested persons. Each person retains a lawyer, as well as a team of other professionals who are neutral, usually a financial professional, at least one mental health professional, and sometimes a child specialist. This method consists of a series of non-confrontational meetings, between each spouse and each neutral professional, between each spouse and his or her attorney, sometimes between both spouses and each neutral professional, and almost always of the full team, that is to say all of the professionals, neutrals, lawyers, and both spouses.

Divorce discussions usually focus first on agreeing how those negotiations should occur. Understanding the different process options is an important first step in resolving your divorce as inexpensively, stresslessly, and quickly as possible.

MISTAKE #2
EMPTYING THE JOINT ACCOUNTS

Some lawyers encourage their clients to clean out the bank accounts "before your spouse does it." This is a declaration of war, equivalent to pushing the red button.

In many jurisdictions, when one person petitions for divorce, the judge enters a standing temporary order, instructing the parties not to dissipate marital assets, not to take all the money and run, etc. The one who unilaterally empties the joint bank accounts will lose credibility in the judge's eyes. If your matter ends up in trial, the judge will be the decision-maker, and you want him or her to view you favorably. Furthermore, your spouse will know that assets are missing and will inevitably embark on a search mission to find the assets. This will cost you both more in attorney's fees and costs of discovery (of information, documents, etc.), and it will delay the conclusion of your case.

Additionally, you and your spouse accumulated your marital assets together, even if you made a marital decision for one of you to stay at home. You are usually not entitled to more than 50% of the marital assets, so you will eventually be forced to return them. In the meantime, by hiding the assets, you will have completely destroyed your relationship with your ex, and perhaps with your children. In a divorce, it is important to see the bigger picture and to understand that there is life after divorce. You don't want to destroy your relationships because of the inappropriate way you acted while your marriage was dissolving.

If you are truly worried, dig up and copy your family's most recent financial information. Inventory and photograph your family's valuables. Move 50% of the liquid funds into an individual account, and don't forget to meet with a financial planner, afterwards.

MISTAKE #3
TALKING TRASH

You may feel you must vent about your issues with the ex. If you do, beware the natural and logical consequences of your actions. The only truly confidential exchange you have is with your lawyer. And that's protected only if there are no outsiders present when you have it.

NEVER trash your ex to your kids. It will hurt you in court, if you insist on going there. And it will certainly bite you back with the children for years to come. Your kids will tell your spouse the bad things that you are saying about him or her. Or, based on the things that come out of your youngsters' mouths, your spouse will know that you are speaking about him or her disparagingly.

I had a horrible case in which the opposing party, the mother, falsely accused my client of sexually molesting their six-year-old daughter. Luna was clearly coaching little Angel to believe that she had been abused. One day, Angel told her grandmother over the phone that "someone is touching my private parts." Her grandmother could hear Luna tell Angel "Don't tell her that! You're not supposed to say that to her!" Additionally, Angel informed Alejandro, "Daddy, I can't go with you until I tell the judge what you did to me." And later, she told him, "you gotta stop touching my private parts, ok, daddy? If you just admit what you did then I can see you."

Needless to say, we obtained 100% timesharing for this father, and their mother didn't see any of their three children for over a year!

I also had a client whose ex began a relationship with a woman, Marcy, who attempted to alienate my client from her young daughter. Among other horrid behavior, the opposing party and Marcy spoke badly about my client in front of little Susie. They would both tell Susie everything that was going on in the court proceedings and that my client was trying to get a judge to try to take her away from her father. This greatly upset Susie, and when it came time for trial, the judge was not happy to hear it.

If you must, vent in the journal that your lawyer should have asked you to maintain.

MISTAKE #4
POSTING ON SOCIAL MEDIA

It's hugely tempting to brag about your new life before you're even divorced, to ensure that your ex knows that you're *over* him or her. Don't post anything that might be used against you! Details about the keg you finished all by yourself, comments about the one-night stands you've enjoyed, pictures of you with your new girlfriend or beau, will not help your divorce case. Consider all of the famous folks who are now infamous idiots just because they *had* to hit "enter."

I had a case where a domestic violence injunction was entered against my client early in the proceedings. Although he was a hothead, I don't believe he was truly physically violent with his wife. Nevertheless, the injunction was entered, and I advised my client to be on his best behavior. Thereafter, Dick began posting pictures on Facebook of him on lavish boats with different women. This infuriated his ex. But the icing on the cake occurred when Dick posted a quote by the Chinese philosopher and reformer, Confucius, "Before you embark on a journey of revenge, dig two graves." Although Dick meant that no good comes from revenge and you will hurt yourself as much as the person you are trying to hurt, his ex claimed that she felt threatened by the quote. She felt that Dick was warning her that he was digging her grave. The judge agreed with her interpretation and extended the domestic violence injunction for another year.

I had a post-paternity action in which the father was seeking additional timesharing with his child. He had begun a relationship with a very young woman, and he wanted to play house. His girlfriend, Hayley, began posting pictures of the parties' kindergarten daughter, Sally, on the internet. The opposing party did nothing to prevent it. Hayley placed captions below these pictures referring to Sally as her own daughter. She even endangered the young girl by creating a "Myspace" page for Sally. The page included pictures of Sally, and references to Sally's school and the city in which she lived when residing with her father. When it came time for trial, the judge did not appreciate these social media posts, and they were a big part of why the judge refused to allow the father more time with Sally.

MISTAKE #5
FILING FALSE CHARGES

Telling the cops that your spouse hit you is not the right way to announce that you want a divorce or to get him or her out of the house. It's a declaration of war, and your kids and bank accounts will suffer in the ensuing firestorm.

I had a client who was granted an injunction, despite that the judge stated in his ruling that "if I had to sit as a jury and find that a battery occurred beyond a reasonable doubt, I don't think I could." In that situation, the parties were fighting, and my client was using her husband's computer without his permission. Unfortunately for him, he put his hands on top of my client's hands and removed them from the keyboard. My client was granted temporary majority timesharing, and, as generally happens, when it came time for the final hearing, the judge did the easy thing and simply made the temporary timesharing final.

In another case, the opposing party, Lizzie, filed her request for a temporary injunction and then quickly dismissed it. She was having an affair and wanted a divorce. A few weeks later, the parties had friends over for dinner and drinks. After their friends left, a drunk Lizzie went to get ready for bed, slipped on the hardwood floor, and hit her head hard on the bed post. She was bleeding badly, and she came out to the kitchen to tell my client.

Gil was extremely concerned, but Lizzie wanted to go to bed. Gil tried to insist that she go to the hospital, but she refused. He restrained her by the wrists so that he could convince her that she needed medical attention. She needed stitches, and he was concerned that she might have a concussion and should not go to sleep. The parties verbally fought about it. Gil called their neighbors, their close friends, for assistance in getting Lizzie to the hospital. They agreed she needed medical attention, and they finally convinced her to go to the hospital.

Lizzie returned to the house that night and spent the night with Gil. She stayed at the house the next day and night with Gil, and then filed her new request for an injunction against him on

Monday morning. As often happens, Lizzie was granted temporary majority timesharing. The parties were eventually able to settle their divorce, but my client had to agree to much less permanent timesharing than he would have liked because of the injunction.

It may sound like this is the best option; after all, these spouses got what they wanted in the short term, didn't they? Come back ten years later. The two families are strikingly similar; in both cases, the kids (every single one of them), as they reached their middle teen years, have moved in with my clients.

Instead of filing a baseless or untruthful injunction, be brave; talk with your spouse about a divorce at the kitchen table. Or invite your spouse to coffee in a public place to have the discussion. You can ask family or a close friend to help you have that talk. Or ask your attorney to help you have that talk.

MISTAKE #6
NOT GETTING A SECOND OPINION

A lawyer should explain the various options available for obtaining that final judgment. But lawyers are human. They have biases. They make mistakes. They want to make money. Always get a second opinion before choosing an attorney. But once you do retain counsel, take her advice!

Most attorneys prefer a certain process, like litigation, mediation, or collaboration. A trial attorney may not understand that she should explain all divorce process options to you so that you can choose the best alternative for you. And if she is not collaboratively-trained, she won't be able to effectively explain that process.

It is important to understand all of your options, so it is best to interview several attorneys. Further, attorneys have different personalities. Some are bulldogs, wanting to go to war over almost every issue. Some attorneys are natural negotiators and more comfortable trying to get you to come to a reasonable settlement.

Moreover, you're going to spend a lot of time with your attorney, so if possible, it is crucial to hire one whom you actually like, and who shares your values. No matter what process you choose, your attorney will be your teammate, and your team will be more successful if you get along with one another.

MISTAKE #7
NOT HIRING A COLLABORATIVE LAWYER

A collaborative divorce will save you time and money, prevent emotional trauma to you and the ones you love, ensure personalized results with which your family can live, and protect your relationships with the people about whom you care. While most divorce processes address only the legal and financial separation between the parties, CP addresses the emotional element of the dissolution of your marriage, as well.

Professionals work as a team to help you resolve your divorce. In many states, the team consists of an attorney for each spouse, a neutral mental health facilitator, and a neutral financial professional. In others, the financial facilitator is supported by an attorney and a mental health coach for each spouse, as well as a child specialist. All team members should be specially-trained in the collaborative paradigm, although a team may agree to the participants' choice of a professional not yet collaboratively trained, if they believe that they can work with the clients' nominee and that he will contribute to a successful collaboration.

Collaborative meetings are intended to be non-confrontational, and to focus on the shared primary goal of finding acceptable resolution between the spouses. Like the neutral team members, collaborative lawyers are trained to work with one another and the clients to manage communications, to ensure that each client is heard, and to explore each issue and possible solution fully. The process does not rely on court-imposed resolutions but instead permits the participants to negotiate in a safe and structured atmosphere of honesty, cooperation, integrity, and professionalism geared toward the future well-being of the restructured family.

The clients pledge to open and transparent communication as between themselves, but private and confidential exchange of information as to the public.

The critical element of the collaborative process that distinguishes it from any other is that the collaborative attorneys must withdraw and the spouses retain separate trial attorneys if any adversarial proceedings ensue. This assures that everyone involved is committed solely to the collaboration and its goals; no one splits his or her attention between collaborating and preparing for litigation in the event that the process terminates.

While participants may be more comfortable with the idea that they will not lose their attorneys if they cannot reach a settlement, the fact that the clients cannot easily opt for litigation means that reaching a settlement is more likely in the collaborative model.

Furthermore, while there are many ethical lawyers out there, many simply do not understand that we all have a conflict with our clients; we want to make money and our clients want to save money. The collaborative process eradicates most of this conflict by eliminating the lawyer's ability to "stir the pot," whether by design or by accident. The lawyer's sole job in the collaborative process is to help the clients satisfy their interests and settle their divorce. If he fails in that task and the collaboration terminates, then he loses his job, and the participants litigate.

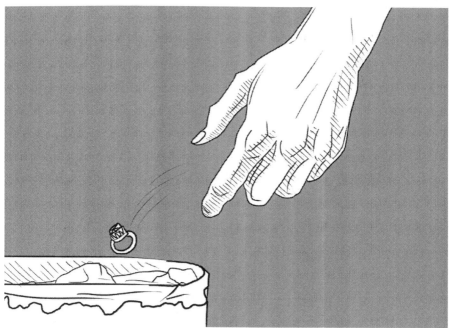

Think Before You Do Something You'll Regret

Every lawyer (except those with a contingency agreement) has a conflict of interest with every one of his clients; the lawyer wants to make more money and the client wants to pay less money. It's a very simple algorithm. Even the most ethical of lawyers suffers from this conflict; it can't be eliminated, although the ethical trial lawyer can certainly avoid its impact on his practice.

In collaborative practice, this conflict is reduced as much as conceivably possible by aligning the client's interests with those of his lawyer. Both are solely concerned with reaching an agreement that satisfies the client. There would be no purpose to the lawyer either concealing information from his client or encouraging his client to feel disserved by the process.

The Florida Bar, as well as others, requires its members to provide their clients with any settlement offers that the other side may make in their case. Monitoring adherence to this obligation is difficult at best. What follows is the story of one lawyer who flaunted the rule and the result when her client discovered her deceit.

I've Been Served

I've been served!

We've all watched legal TV shows and seen the process server knock on the door and announce dramatically, "you've been served!" while thrusting a sheaf of paperwork at the defendant. I'm a family lawyer, so, like any sane attorney, I know that I never want to sue anyone or to be sued by anyone. I know better than to "go to court." (No one wins in court.)

But I *have* been sued. Yes, I have. I once had a gal come see me who'd been in her divorce case for over a year. She finally fired her lawyer, consulted with me, and asked me to take over her case.

After she retained me, I contacted the opposing counsel and asked, "Ron, I was reviewing Jane Doe's file and I noticed that she didn't have any correspondence in the file about any settlement offers. But her case is so simple, knowing you, I figured you'd have made an offer early on. Didn't you?"

"Well, yes, of course, I did, Joryn. But I never heard back from her lawyer. So I dropped it."

"Can you send me a copy?"

"Sure I can." And he did.

I called my client into my office and sat her down. "Jane, have you ever seen this letter before?" She looked a little startled, but I could understand why. The letter was addressed to her former counsel and was over a year old. It was only a page long but she read it carefully. I waited. Then she read it again.

"No," she replied, clearly confused.

I explained what had obviously happened; Ron had sent her lawyer an offer to settle and she had never sent it on to Jane. This, by the way, was a violation of The Florida Bar rules, which require lawyers to communicate settlement offers to their clients.

Jane was appalled. I asked if she wanted to accept the offer, assuming that it was still available (which Ron had assured me that it was). "Oh, my, yes! I would have accepted it last year, had I known!"

I settled Jane's case. But that's not where this story ends. One evening soon thereafter, a process server showed up at my house and served me with what we call a "third party complaint"! Apparently, Jane had sued her erstwhile attorney for legal malpractice. (Her complaint read "She negligently failed to send me the settlement letter.") The lawyer then sued me, alleging that it was my fault that Jane had never received Ron's settlement offer.

What?! Anybody can sue anyone for anything.

I had to notify my legal malpractice insurance carrier of the lawsuit. My rate jumped from $8,000/year to $18,000/year. For the next five years. I answered the complaint, and never had to do another thing; Jane and her former lawyer settled their case without my involvement.

In fact, it was not an accident; it was not negligence. She had done it on purpose. She is one of those family lawyers who prefer that the litigation continue for as long as possible; that's how she makes her money.

Nearly every lawyer has a conflict of interest with every single client; the lawyer wants to make money (to be paid by the client), but the client wants to save money (to pay the lawyer as little as possible).

Quiz — Is Collaborative Divorce Right For You?

Take this quiz if you are considering getting divorced:

1.   Do you love your children more than anything else in the world?

2.   Do you have limited funds to spend on lawyers, experts, depositions, and other litigation expenses?

3.   Do you loathe face-to-face confrontations and hurting other people's feelings for no good reason?

4.   Do you value your privacy and resent having other people knowing your personal business?

5.   Do you appreciate being able to make the decisions that affect your life without interference from a governmental third-party?

6.   Do you hate it when others delay making decisions that you need to be made so that you can get on with your life?

7.   Do you despise people who gossip about you without knowing the real facts?

8.   Do you want to be able to take vacations with your kids without worrying about whether a judge will permit you to do so?

9.   Do you miss those good old days when you and your spouse used to be on the same page about everything?

10. Do you want to be divorced without causing pain to your family, your friends, your neighbors, and everyone else you care about?

11. Would you prefer to part ways with your spouse without hating each other?

If you answered "yes" to 0-3 of these questions, then you are an unlikely candidate for a collaborative divorce and the traditional courtroom route is recommended for you.

If you answered "yes" to 4-7 of these questions, then you are a candidate for a collaborative divorce, and you may be successful in that process.

If you answered "yes" to 8-11 of these questions, then you are a prime candidate for the collaborative process and have a high probability of concluding that process successfully.

Navigating the Divorce Process

CHAPTER FOUR
Choose Your Fate: Collaborate!

Divorce proceedings usually stir up emotion and distress. The breakdown of a marriage is often traumatic and full of drama. Adding overly litigious attorneys to the mix can push already strained relationships over the edge. The collaborative process is a dignified alternative approach to the dissolution of the marriage which offers the couple a way to resolve their issues outside of the courtroom. By opening up the lines of communication, by sharing information, by collaboratively problem-solving, and by using interest-based negotiation techniques, participants work to reach a mutually acceptable settlement agreement that fashions results based on the highest and true priorities of each spouse.

CP is a solution-oriented approach that emphasizes the effects of divorce on children and the quality of life for all family members after divorce. It provides many attractions to the normal person. Couples often feel more confident with this process because they receive the guidance of neutral professionals in whom they can both repose trust, and of their own counsels, who advocate on their behalves, but in a non-adversarial and collaborative fashion. In some communities, they each have their own coaches, as well. Thus, they avoid the mudslinging common to litigated divorces.

Many couples, especially those with children, must continue their relationships post-divorce; it benefits them to place the dissolution of their marriage relationship in a supportive and safe environment during the process. In addition, collaborative clients don't leave their fates to a judge who doesn't know them or their kids, or share their values, and who sees a snapshot of their lives. Moreover, divorce is costly, and the collaborative approach provides a less expensive method of resolving those issues.[3]

The collaborative method requires couples to agree to forego the traditional litigation process that is the default setting for divorce, and instead, to work with professionals to resolve their

---

[3] For a table comparing the cost of a typical collaborative divorce with the expense of a typical traditional courtroom divorce, go to the author's website at www.OpenPalmLaw.com.

issues. At the beginning of the process, the individuals sign a participation agreement which includes a disqualification clause.

What does that mean? If either spouse decides to forego the collaboration, and to proceed with their divorce in court, *both* of their attorneys must withdraw their representation. This DQ provision benefits the divorcing spouses because their entire team, including the lawyers, is truly focused on assisting them to reach a settlement and to avoid court. Because of this pledge, the participants are able to speak freely without worrying that their words may be used against them in court. This creates a "safe" environment in which the team can help both of the participants to negotiate effectively. This also eliminates the tendency of all trial attorneys to "hope for the best, but plan for the worst," i.e. to hope for agreement but plan for trial, which dilutes their efforts in any non-collaborative settlement process.

It also dis-incentivizes either spouse from pulling the plug and being required to retain new counsel.

Because the commitment not to go to court is a formal agreement rather than just a promise, it builds trust, which helps both clients get the results they want. The pledge incentivizes participants to work towards a settlement rather than giving up on the collaborative choice, falling back on the courtroom option, and surrendering their attorneys. This is a positive force, chosen by the participants—because in the vast majority of cases, reaching a collaborative settlement is a better alternative than relying on a judge to render a fair judgment that works for both of them.

In addition, CP eliminates the lawyer's ability to "stir the pot," which many do accidentally and some do by design. The lawyer's sole job in the collaborative model is to help the clients satisfy their interests and settle their divorce.

A key element is the transparency promise, the agreement by the participants that they will share information and openly communicate with each other. If a participant declines to disclose relevant information, and after attempting to convince him to do so he still refuses, his attorney must bow out from the process. The pledge to be transparent not only helps the clients to trust one another so that they can effectively negotiate, but it saves time and money because the clients are not required to hunt down documents and engage in traditional courtroom "discovery."

The collaborative team helps the participants to negotiate their interests, rather than their positions. If a party insists on a specific outcome, she is taking a position, rather than negotiating an interest. If the other party takes the opposite position, they deadlock. However, if the clients discuss their underlying interests, they are likely to uncover different outcomes. They will first identify a goal and then brainstorm multiple options to meet that goal, rather than a single option that satisfies only one position.

When determining whether collaborative practice is appropriate, it is crucial to evaluate expectations and the ability to listen to the needs of the other participant. CP only works if all participants participate with honesty. Couples must act with maturity and respect. Many divorcing clients find this requirement especially challenging because there is so much emotion involved. But a good collaborative team will guide them to focus on their most important issues. The participants should appreciate that they are working together, rather than against one another.

Once the clients have agreed to proceed with the collaborative method, their attorneys will assemble other professionals for assistance. Sometimes they retain a mental health professional to work with the participants, both separately and together—not as a therapist, but as a facilitator to teach the clients to more effectively communicate, to problem solve, and to co-parent successfully. Sometimes they will each retain a mental health coach instead.

They are also likely to retain a financial professional. This nonaligned team member will prepare budgets and asset and liability reports, and may fashion equitable distribution and support schedules, if desired and appropriate. If there is no neutral mental health professional to lead the team, then the financial neutral will probably perform that function, as well

The team may also hire other impartial professionals. Child specialists who focus on the developmental stages of children may help the participants to hear the concerns and interests of their children, and to develop their parenting plan. Valuation experts may value businesses. Appraisers may value assets or real estate. Financial planners may advise the clients as to how best to manage the funds and assets that they plan to receive in their divorce.

Prior to each meeting, the attorneys will confer with their own clients and with the rest of the team to determine the agenda. The team professionals will determine the optimum means to ensure that the meeting runs effectively and that the issues are strategically raised at the best possible times.

During meetings, the team will assign tasks to the participants that they must perform before the next meeting so that each party has full knowledge of the issues. Often, the team will ask the clients to sign the minutes or the notes taken at each meeting.

After each meeting, the attorneys will meet with their respective clients to obtain feedback and to answer questions. The entire team will also meet to debrief and for constructive criticism.

This innovative practice method offers a means to decrease the expense of divorce, while helping divorcing spouses maintain their relationships once it is concluded. Any participant who wishes to maintain a cordial bond with his or her spouse after their divorce, and who wants to maximize his or her chances of reaching a settlement that addresses their most important interests, should consider the benefits of collaborative divorce.

An Open Palm Holds More Than a Closed Fist

When we witness acts of cruelty, deception, or immoral behavior there is a palpable feeling deep down that is gut wrenching and tangible. We all know what that feeling is, and we know what it screams out for: justice. We can understand when justice seems required, but what is the actual nature of justice?

The Judge

Justice in the form of a universal ideology has escaped even the greatest philosophers and thinkers for the last 2500 years. We know justice exists, but in the abstract form it is more elemental than substantial. We know it exists through some innate power of reason, but understand it cannot be physically measured or weighed. From Plato to Aristotle, to Hobbes, Hume, Locke, and Rousseau, all have failed to form a satisfactory over-arching definition of justice.

In Plato's *The Republic*, Plato's brother Glaucon challenged Socrates to define justice. Glaucon discusses the legend of Gyges, who discovered a ring that gave him the power to become invisible. With his ring, Gyges enters the palace, seduces the Queen, and kills the king, ultimately claiming the throne for himself. Thus no man would be just if he had the opportunity to perpetrate injustice with impunity. The only reason that men are just is out of fear of being punished for injustice. The law is a compromise between individuals who agree not to do injustice to others if others will not do injustice to them. Glaucon argues that if people had the power to do injustice without fear of reprisal, they would not enter into such an agreement.

Jean-Jacques Rousseau maintains in *The Social Contract*, that, in a well-ordered society, the general will (rather than the wants of any individual or group of individuals) must prevail. True freedom in society requires following the general will, and those who do not choose to can legitimately be forced to do so.

David Hume, on the other hand, felt that justice was a trumped up social constraint enforced to maintain the illusion of property rights.

Still don't understand what justice is? You're not alone. Justice may be black-and-white to some, while for others, their perception of justice can at times be radically different than our own. The following story describes what *should* have been a black-and-white courtroom result, but was not, purely because the judge allowed her personal interests to impact her decision-making.

John Hammer was nineteen when he first walked into my office, some twenty years ago. He was a gangly, sandy-haired kid dressed in jeans and a t-shirt despite the chill January outside. His flip flops flapped against his heels as Valerie conducted him down the hallway into the conference room. He had brought his father, a tall silver-haired man dressed in a dark suit and red tie, to the consultation.

I had opened my law practice six months before, but I was already fourteen years in the profession — both practicing law in various law firms, and, at one point, teaching law full-time as a professor at Stetson University College of Law in St. Petersburg, Florida.

It was a lawsuit that brought them to see me. They were both upset, but I think John's father, Adrian, was more perturbed. I suspected he was worried, when John professed ignorance of what the litigation was about, that his son was lying.

While John was a sophomore at the University of Florida, in Gainesville, his car was towed. He emerged from class one day to find it gone, vanished from his paid parking slot. Fresh-faced and naïve, he tried to retrieve it from the impound lot. The faceless clerk told him it would cost $2500, $500 more than he had paid for it the month before. John was flabbergasted. The clerk continued, "Your car was levied on to satisfy a final judgment entered against you." She gave him a copy of the judgment entered by a court in Hillsborough County.

John was stymied, so he did what any normal American kid would do; he called his dad for help. He had no idea what the lawsuit was about, nor did his father. They wanted me to find out and fix it.

The file was thin but I reviewed it carefully. It appeared that a complaint had been filed against John in small claims court for damage done to a motor vehicle he had rented. The complaint was brief, just one short count (or claim) for breach of contract. The car rental company, a business called *Rent-A-Ruin*, had obtained a judgment against him for the damage when he failed to answer their complaint.

Why had John not answered it? I made an appointment to discuss this with him. He returned with his father.

"John, have you ever heard of a company called *Rent-A-Ruin*?"

John turned towards me. "Yeah, I think that was the place I rented a car from to go back up to school after summer break. It broke down about halfway back to Gainesville. I had to thumb my way back from there."

My first thought was that this poor kid had not had the sense to contact the leasing company to report the problem with the vehicle. Silly me! John had called the *Rent-A-Ruin* customer service desk as soon as he arrived back at school (no cell phones back then, at least not for college kids).

"What did they tell you?"

"The lady said not to worry, she would send somebody to pick up the car right away."

"Did you get her name?"

He had not, but that wasn't really the problem. The file demonstrated what the real problem was, at least initially. Although John had never been notified that a lawsuit had been filed against him, a process server had filed an affidavit, confirming he had served John with the complaint for damages to the vehicle. Because John had never answered, the court had entered a default judgment against him.

I pulled out the service of process form completed by the process server, whose name I did not recognize, and handed it to John. "Do you know the address where you were supposedly served?"

"Of course I do. I worked there last summer. It's the *Macaroni Grill* on North Dale Mabry."

"And you're telling me that you were never served?" I pointed to the complaint still sitting on the edge of my desk before him.

"No!" He examined it closely. "I've never seen this before."

I moved the court to set the final judgment against John Hammer aside. The reason I gave was that he had never been served with the complaint, but making the motion was just the beginning of my work. I had to find out what had really happened.

57

As it turned out, John had allegedly been served while working as a waiter at the local restaurant. It was a summer job. He was no longer working there by the time the complaint had been served. He had already returned to Gainesville for the fall semester, driving the rented "ruin" at least part of the way.

I went to lunch. There was a *Macaroni Grill* just down the street from my office, but I wasn't interested in food. Instead, I drove to the restaurant where my client had spent the summer and asked for the manager. He soon appeared and I invited him to join me at my table.

I interviewed him. He was new, but had been there on the date the complaint was served and already knew the story; he clarified that it had been another employee who had actually been served, another waiter whose first name was also, coincidentally, "John."

Thankfully, John Adams happened to be on shift while I was meeting with his boss. The manager called him over.

Adams informed me that, at the end of September the year before, he had been called to the front of the restaurant by the hostess. The hostess, a pretty young thing, had gestured to an unremarkable middle-aged guy who stood there with a sheaf of papers in his hand. "He wants to talk to you."

"Can I help you?" John had asked.

"Are you John?" the man abruptly replied, without bothering to introduce himself.

"Yes, I am. How can I help you?"

Instead of responding, the stranger handed him the sheaf of papers and announced, without further explanation, "You are served."

John immediately inspected the documents and realized the man being sued was a different "John." He had called the attorney who had signed the complaint, as the subpoena suggested, using the phone in the manager's office. He had notified the lawyer that he was not the John Hammer who was being sued. According to him, the attorney had callously replied, "Too bad."

At that point, the eighteen-year old, having done all he could, had hung up the phone and dismissed the matter from his mind. He didn't know John Hammer and he wasn't the one in trouble. In fact, he'd never met my client, having been hired after John

Hammer had returned to Gainesville.

The attorney went ahead and obtained a judgment against my client, who only discovered this fact when his car was seized.

The judge granted my request for an evidentiary hearing on our motion to set the judgment aside because of the mistake. At the hearing, I introduced four witnesses: my client, who testified that he had never been served; John Adams, who testified that he *had* been served and had called the lawyer to put him on notice that he was not the "John" named in the complaint; the prior manager of the *Macaroni Grill*, who had been in charge the summer that John Hammer was employed; and the current manager, who had taken over at the end of the summer, had employed John Adams, and had suggested that Adams call the attorney to explain the situation when he was mistakenly served.

Of course, the attorney for *Rent-A-Ruin* put the process server on the stand, but he only testified that he served the papers on the person who responded when he went to the place of employment and asked for "John." He explained that he serves dozens of people every day and can't be expected to remember them all. Nor did we; that's why the affidavit.

If there was ever a slam-dunk, this was it. The judge would *have* to grant the motion to set aside and permit my client to defend the suit against him for breach of contract. He would be allowed to explain that the rental car had broken down before he reached school.

At the end of the hearing, the judge announced her ruling; "I deny the motion." I know my mouth fell open. She concluded with the following admonition to my witnesses, forever etched into my aural memory: "I find that you people are mistaken, and that John Hammer was, in fact, served with the complaint."

Adrian, who had witnessed the entire hearing, joined us as we filed out of the courtroom, appalled. Thank goodness he had seen it for himself. I was unable to explain what had happened. They both knew that if there was ever a black-and-white case, this was it. But we had still lost.

It was years later that I discovered that the judge, the lawyer for *Rent-A-Ruin*, and the process server were all good friends. The lawyer and the process server appeared regularly in the judge's courtroom.

And that, as Paul Harvey used to say, is "the rest of the story."

Except that it's not. John Hammer and John Adams both learned that day, firsthand, that the justice system often simply does not work.

The judicial system is administered by human beings; human beings work in it and on it, and it is therefore permeated with human error and other less admirable traits. If you imagine that it is fair and impartial and just, and that you can always get the "fair" result, then you are sadly mistaken and possibly misguided.

Don't put your divorce in the hands of a judge who may be having a bad day, who may have values different from yours, or who may have a hidden agenda. Use the collaborative method, or at least a courtless option, take control of the decisions in your divorce, and settle whatever differences you may have *outside* the courtroom.

Judges Are Human, Too!

When a jury or judge hears a case and makes a decision that might impact you for the rest of your life, the outcome is never predictable. You've all heard the old saying "it all depends on what the judge had for breakfast," or "it all depends on which side of the bed the judge woke up on." Here is a story about the jury rendering an unexpected verdict in a case in which the defendant and his attorney were certain of the outcome.

Another reason why collaborative divorce is a great idea. No surprises.

Guilty

I was what we call "a baby lawyer" when I tried my first case in front of a jury. At twenty-six, I worked as an assistant state attorney. I had moved up through the Intake Division into Traffic. The judge was a stern-looking middle-aged white man who rarely smiled. His judicial assistant looked like she snacked on lemons. In contrast, the bailiff, clad in forest green was a tall, black, former sheriff who welcomed me into his courtroom. He was quick to explain the rules, so that I didn't embarrass myself. I was grateful.

The defendant was accused of driving under the influence, and my opposing counsel was the number one DUI attorney in town, Vincent Perotti.

This took place in 1983, and the years have erased my memory of the underlying facts. But I vividly recall interviewing potential jurors. I had carefully crafted the questions to assist my choices from the jury venire, the pool of potential jurors. I inquired about their backgrounds and possible prejudices. I asked if they would be able to apply the law to the facts of the case impartially. At the end, the judge gestured for Vincent and me to approach the bench. There, out of their earshot, we could exercise our strikes and remove potential jurors we didn't want.

I could tell that both the judge and Vincent were waiting for me to seize the opportunity to get rid of three, two men and a woman. The decision rested on me; I had no one second-chairing the case. It was obvious why. The first man had been convicted of DUI ten years before. The second man had been convicted of DUI five years before. And the woman's husband had been arrested for

DUI six months before. Logic said to strike them all.

But my gut told me to leave them, so I did.

I don't recall actually trying the case; I *do* remember being very nervous. I *do* recollect it took less than two hours. And I *do* recall our closing arguments. Mine seemed so brief. Vincent, on the other hand, went on at great length about all the gaps in my evidence.

Those jurors filed out of the courtroom like little ducklings behind their green-suited mother duck to the privacy of the jury room. And I remember the shock on the bailiff's face when they all filed back into the courtroom less than seven minutes later.

I had never before experienced the formalized protocol of obtaining the verdict from the foreman of the jury and publishing it. It seemed to take forever. Finally, the judicial assistant read from the sheet of paper that had been handed up to her. "Guilty!"

The bailiff grinned broadly at me.

I didn't look at the defendant's expression, but the shock on Vincent's face was palpable. The bailiff ushered the jury out to wherever juries go, and the judge swept out his own door with his minions, his black robes flying behind him.

It took several minutes for Vincent and me to pack up our briefcases. I was hurt when he ignored the hand I held out to shake his prior to exiting the courtroom.

I shouldn't have been. My new friend, the bailiff, had returned just to inform me that mine was the fastest guilty verdict in the history of Hillsborough County.

Years later, I mused out the reason for the swift guilty verdict. It was crystal clear: the two guys convicted of DUI? They knew in their hearts that they were guilty, and, if they had to pay the piper, then so did my defendant. The gal whose husband had been arrested? She knew that her husband was guilty. In fact, she was probably in the car with him when he was arrested. I'd bet dollars to donuts that she had offered to drive instead of him, but he had turned her down. And if he had to pay the piper, then so did my guy!

We can ponder how the judge or jury makes decisions all day long. We can hire jury consultants to help us anticipate how jury members will react to the evidence and to the way we present it.

But, at the end of the day, we can never be certain. I can only confirm that trial work is an art, not a science, and that my gut was right when Vincent's head was wrong that day in 1983.

Trial Work is Exciting... For the Lawyer

Once again, I see how the collaborative process actually brings people back together in their relationship, even as they end the legality of their marriage. This is critical for folks who must remain co-parents for life. In this case, I was struck by the possibility that my client might never have known why her husband had become "so selfish" if she had not chosen to proceed collaboratively. And that would have been tragic, not just for her, but for him and — more importantly — for the two children they share.

The Secret

Tampa's Bay Area Legal Services recently referred Tabitha Jamison to me for help with her divorce. Tabitha is a matronly woman of color, with striking clear green eyes, whose face is usually crinkled in a radiant smile. She is habitually dressed in a professional-looking pants suit. Because she only makes $8,800 a year and lives in a leased apartment, she qualifies for *pro bono* services.

After I explained her options — the kitchen table divorce, the mediated divorce, and the traditional courtroom brawl, among others — she opted for the collaborative choice. She explained that she and Mr. Jamison had been separated for over twelve years. Although he had had two more children by two different women during those years, and she believed that his current girlfriend might be pregnant, they had continued while separated to co-parent their own two children amicably. She saw no reason why their divorce should change that.

Chuck Jamison makes approximately $60,000 a year, he has five children by four different women, and his current girlfriend is pregnant. All of his children live with their mothers, but he spends substantial amounts of time with each. He religiously maintains his child support payments.

The standards of our practice group's *pro bono* committee permit me to make the judgment call, so I found him a lawyer who was willing to take his part on a *pro bono* basis, as well. Chuck agreed to participate with Tabitha on a collaborative basis in their divorce. His lawyer, Eric, and I chose the facilitator, Melinda, and the neutral financial professional, Tanya, and both of them agreed to volunteer their time.

The clients each met with both Melinda and Tanya. The professional team and our shadows (professionals trained collaboratively but who had not yet handled a collaborative divorce themselves) held a conference call thereafter to discuss the case details as we each understood them. Thus, the facilitator shared with us her perspective on the wife's anger, caused by her perception of her husband's recent selfishness. Over the last few years, he'd been less forthcoming when she asked for extra money towards the children's expenses.

Her irritation came to a head because their daughter was turning sixteen and wanted a special *Sweet Sixteen* party. Tabitha's research showed it would cost $2500 for the party venue that her daughter wanted, and that was more than she could pay. Her anger rose when she approached Chuck to discuss it. He simply said that he couldn't afford to help her and failed to even offer to contribute. Until recently he had never been so close-mouthed; they used to be able to talk about everything. She didn't know what had changed, but she was fed up!

During our first full team meeting, we reviewed the particulars of the collaborative participation agreement[4] and ensured that everyone present — the shadows, as well as the entire working team — had executed it. We identified the clients' interests, which were not complicated. There was no personal property to distribute, no home to argue over, and their long separation left neither asking for alimony.

Nevertheless, we proceeded judiciously. Our team had never worked together before, and we were cautious; we didn't know what the team dynamic would be yet and we wanted to ensure that we were communicating and collaborating well together.

Tabitha explained that her number one interest was providing higher education for their two children. No one in either her family or in Chuck's had attended college, including his oldest son by his first wife who was now nineteen. She appreciated that Chuck had already had lengthy discussions with their two children about the advantages of higher education. Tabitha emphasized her regret

---

[4] A sample collaborative participation agreement can be found on the author's website at www.OpenPalmLaw.com.

and frustration that she had never been able to go. She beamed when she told us how well her sixteen-year-old girl and fourteen-year-old boy had done in school. Despite the daughter's near-blindness, she believed they both would continue to excel beyond high school.

Tabitha did not mention, at this point, that she wanted Chuck to increase her child support. Because his earlier-born child, a nineteen-year-old, was no longer in school or legally entitled to his support, she believed this was fair. She did emphasize that Chuck was a wonderful father, always available for parent-teacher conferences, always available to be the disciplinarian when she needed his support, always there for their kids, and always understanding of both their children and of her.

This led to her concern over Chuck's inexplicable selfishness, particularly regarding the *Sweet Sixteen* party. Melinda ensured that Tabitha was able to fully express her feelings about this issue and that she had no other interests that she wanted to cover. Only then did she ask Chuck to express his interests.

Chuck was the same age as Tabitha, but he looked older. He was a handsome man, and also dressed in business casual—a nice pair of trousers and a golf shirt, with a closely cropped haircut and a clean-shaven face. He did not smile when he explained what a wonderful mother Tabitha was now, had always been, and how much he valued that in her. He completely affirmed her desire to have their kids go to college and earn bachelor's degrees. That would make him very happy.

However, he emphasized, his primary concern was to ensure that his children were *citizens* of the United States. They were growing up in the best country on earth, at the best time possible, and he wanted so very much for them to *be* citizens. That meant that they would make a contribution, that they would understand that *they* were important, and that *they* could make a difference.

His passionate comments generated a long pause around the table. At this point his attorney asked if Chuck would feel comfortable sharing what they had discussed in their off-line meeting earlier in the week. Chuck hesitated for a long moment before he said, "Yes." He then turned in his chair slightly, but noticeably (to me, at least) away from Tabitha and myself towards

Eric and Melinda, the facilitator.

He looked down at the surface of the table for another lengthy silence, and then began, "I never thought I'd have to say this." He paused. "But I know what it's like to be *America's Most Wanted*." He continued to face Eric and Melinda; he avoided addressing Tabitha. "I had a great job with the railroad. But a few years ago, I was laid off. So I applied for unemployment."

Tabitha nodded; she remembered.

"My unemployment insurance helped me pay the bills, but it couldn't cover all of my child support, as well." He paused again. "I hoped the railroad would rehire me, or find me another job, so I continued to look for other positions with the railroad. But it was a long time, and I exhausted my savings just keeping my child support payments current.

"Eventually, I found a part-time job. It was minimum wage but I thought it was better than nothing. The money I made from that job, and other part-time jobs I was able to find, together with my unemployment, allowed me to pay my child support without missing a beat."

Chuck took a deep breath, and continued with his story. Eventually, the railroad rehired him for his old job and his life returned to normal. Throughout this time, none of his children ever lacked for his child support. Then he got the phone call. At first, he didn't grasp its significance; a woman called from the railroad board and asked to meet with him. He set a time outside of business. But then his plans went awry, so he called to postpone and reschedule. When she said, "Let's just meet at the police station," he realized this was more serious than he had understood.

The following series of events blurred together for him. As requested, he went to the police station, where he met with the woman and a federal investigator. They accused him of defrauding the federal government. Unbeknownst to him, his minimum-wage part-time jobs had violated the railroad's unemployment conditions. He had been under the mistaken impression that any part-time position was acceptable as long as it wasn't for the railroad. The federal investigator threatened him with ten years in prison if he didn't plead guilty to fraud for each two-week period that he had reapplied for unemployment while earning money part-time.

Of course, he retained a lawyer, but his limited resources forced him to borrow against his retirement funds in order to pay for legal fees. His attorney recommended that he accept the plea bargain; plead guilty to all twenty-five counts of fraud in exchange for five years of probation and complete restitution. He agreed to pay back all of the unemployment money he had received while he worked part time. With his back against the wall, he had no choice but to sign on the dotted line.

At this point Chuck's eyes were moist. Although he wasn't crying, it took all of my self-control to contain my own tears. And I was not alone.

Then Chuck detailed his fears about being on house arrest while awaiting his sentencing. Would his children know something was wrong when they visited? How could he hide it from them? Would they notice that he wouldn't step outside the front door during their sleepovers? Thankfully, they did not.

At his sentencing hearing, the man preceding him pled guilty to selling two hundred and fifty pounds of cocaine. The man following admitted to setting up a pyramid scheme, defrauding old folks of their retirement funds. When Chuck faced the judge to discuss his plea bargain, he was unable to agree that he was guilty of the crimes with which he'd been charged. The judge was adamant that he should show some remorse. However, Chuck stood his ground. He had not intended to commit fraud; he had simply been ignorant. As a former prosecutor, I realized how lucky Chuck had been. After the judge castigated him far more severely than either the preceding man or the one following him, he approved the negotiated plea bargain.

Chuck will remain on probation until 2018. He is paying the restitution, as well as repaying the retirement fund loan he withdrew to pay his lawyer. With no money to spare, he has no resources to help with the *Sweet Sixteen* celebration. He'd been unable to tell Tabitha why, until now—with the help of our facilitator and the rest of the collaborative team.

At this point, an hour and forty minutes into our first full team meeting, I suggested a break.

Tabitha and I met off-line; I wanted her reaction to Chuck's news outside of the team environment because her body language had signaled extreme anger to me. She was fairly vibrating with fury as she explained that she and Chuck had been friends since high school, and had always been able to talk to each other. She was furious that he had not trusted her enough to confide in her.

When I asked her to trust me; she agreed. I explained that I understood her feelings of betrayal, but asked her to consider his view, to try to stand in his shoes for just a moment.

"Tabitha, I think that preserving your respect for him, and even more importantly, your children's respect for him, was so important to Chuck that he's been unwilling to risk losing it by confiding in you. Now, in this safe environment, he felt that he could tell you."

While she sat deep in thought, I waited for her reaction.

When she finally responded, I knew my words had struck a chord. She acknowledged that his feelings for her were more complex than she had imagined. She agreed to consider the new information and to reassess past events in light of it. I begged her not to confront Chuck in the meantime, but instead to meet with Melinda, our facilitator, to help her process. We went back to the meeting and asked to adjourn until the next full team meeting in a few weeks.

A few days after we adjourned, Melinda sent the following e-mail:

> I spoke with Tabitha today. She is doing fine. She said that she and Chuck actually spoke yesterday after the meeting and processed what happened a little more. Then they went on to discuss Kasey's *Sweet Sixteen*. She said they are in a good place. She thought the meeting went real well.

Here's the thing: the outcome would have been far different with traditional trial attorneys and other litigation-oriented professionals. One result could have included either Tabitha's lawyer uncovering the fact that he is now a felon, or Chuck spilling his guts in the courtroom. Either way, he would have been humiliated by Tabitha's attorney, and undoubtedly his kids would eventually have learned of his embarrassing conviction.

The other possibility is that his conviction would have remained secret, and Tabitha would have continued to believe that he'd simply become a selfish son of a bitch. Either way, their efforts to co-parent effectively would have been tragically compromised, and their children would have lost the benefit of having two congenial parents working in unity together.

Let there be no doubt that proceeding collaboratively was the best option that this couple could have elected. We were now well on our way to helping Tabitha and Chuck finalize the dissolution of their marriage while remaining amicable parents of the children they share, and who still respect them both.

Consider Your Children

Although our clients are technically adults, we often feel like we represent children, and I don't mean the children of the clients. True, divorce is one of the biggest stressors in life, ranking up there with death and taxes. But why does it make so many regress to adolescent immaturity?

This case is a lesson in the cost one can incur when one conceals information from one's own attorney.

The Spouse Swap

Jeremy Lubsen strode into my office for his initial consultation, and announced that he had very little time to afford me. Although he was dressed like a steelworker, he carried his spare 6'2" frame like he owned the steel works. "I don't have a lot of time, so let's make this quick. I want to divorce my wife so that I can marry my pregnant girlfriend." He immediately rubbed me the wrong way, but we don't always like those whom we represent.

I specifically asked, as I always do, "Who referred you to me?" He simply replied "my girlfriend" again, and didn't tell me her name. He certainly neglected to mention that his girlfriend, Rita, was the former wife of an old client of mine, Alex. She had referred Jeremy because, in her opinion, I had performed an exceptional job for her ex-husband (against *her* attorney) during *their* divorce. (It is not unusual that a new client will not tell me that a former "opposing party" referred him to me; the person referring him has usually requested that he not divulge his or her name, for obvious reasons.)

Only later, when I discovered her name, did I realize the connection.

Jeremy hurriedly proceeded with his story. "My wife, Renee, knows I want a divorce. I've already moved out of our home. We've already agreed to a timesharing schedule in which I have the kids overnight every other Friday, Saturday, and Sunday, as well as every Wednesday. So, this should be an easy divorce for you. I just want it over as quickly as possible." I could tell Jeremy likely would not make this an easy process, but I kept my mouth shut, and he retained us.

Throughout the divorce process, Jeremy and Renee each

complained bitterly that the other spoke derogatorily about him or her to their young children and discussed the divorce with the kids. When Jeremy inquired of their admittedly precocious ten-year-old daughter what she wanted for her birthday, she replied "I want you to help Mommy by giving us money." During his stupefied silence while he tried to digest that, she continued, "I also want you to stop using your new girlfriend as bait to lure me to go with you."

On many occasions, their eight-year-old son informed him "Mommy doesn't like you, and neither do I." Despite these statements, the boy's playful actions belied these unsolicited and vitriolic comments. Jeremy, his complexion apoplectic, nearly shouted that he *knew* Renee had planted these words.

Of course, she leveled similar accusations against Jeremy.

Later, his daughter told him that she didn't want to visit with him and that her mother had revealed to her that she "didn't have to." In addition, the child began cross-examining him about a "work trip" to Las Vegas, taken prior to her parents' separation. She asked whether he had brought Rita with him. Because *he* had never discussed this trip with his daughter, clearly Renee had done so.

At the same time as he insisted that we move for an order to show cause why Renee should not be held in contempt of court for her violations of the standard order against involving the children in the litigation, against our advice, he shut off her access to telephone and internet. His daughter asked him why he did it. She then asked him about an upcoming court date.

Although our client was no gem, Renee was clearly defying the temporary standing order which forbids parties from discussing divorce litigation in the presence of the children, much less *with* them.

The Lubsens also created many problems with their timesharing plan. Each regularly changed the schedule without the other's input, much less approval. On one occasion, Jeremy attempted to visit with the children on his usual Wednesday evening, but Renee, who was upset over an unrelated divorce issue, refused to answer the door, and, when he ran an errand to allow her time to cool down, left the county with the children to frustrate his timesharing that night altogether.

During mediation, they agreed that Jeremy would drop the children off at the marital home in the mornings no earlier than one hour before school began. Renee unilaterally decided that he should drop the children off at school instead. If he would not, then he could not share time with them overnight.

One Wednesday, Jeremy and Rita went to Renee's home at the normal exchange time to retrieve the children, but they weren't there. He waited. When they finally arrived, she refused to allow him to take them. At this point, he blocked her car in the driveway with his car so she couldn't leave. The Lubsens engaged in a verbal altercation, and Renee called the police. The children witnessed this entire, unnecessary incident.

Although Jeremy was ultimately allowed to take the children when he showed the cops his timesharing order, the police dislike being involved in civil disputes and will often tell disputants that they're not judges and cannot determine timesharing issues. On this occasion, the police simply convinced Renee to allow Jeremy to take the children.

Renee's threats to withhold the children violated the standing order. It weakened her argument that she should have majority timesharing, because her behavior was simply not in the kids' best interests. Maintaining the set schedule *would* have been in their best interests, providing a sense of stability during the divorce.

However, Jeremy shouldn't have allowed the situation to escalate into a heated disagreement in front of the children.

To protect his time with the children and reduce her involvement, against our advice, he began to take the children from school a half hour early so she couldn't pick them up. Like Renee, Jeremy should have refrained from needlessly changing their routines during this stressful time for them.

Moreover, during his telephone conversations with the children, Renee refused to take Jeremy off the speaker phone, despite that unless the Court orders otherwise, parents are entitled to private conversations with their children. When he confronted her about it, she was very agitated and kept saying that she could do whatever she wanted to do. Her comments about Rita made it clear she was punishing Jeremy because she was upset when she could hear Rita in the background.

They couldn't even communicate civilly via e-mail.

Renee had a small business selling products on E-Bay. Without her permission, he changed all of the information on her E-Bay account and put it in his and Rita's names.

Both of the Lubsens acted immaturely and vindictively toward each other throughout the litigation, always putting their needs ahead of their children's best interests.

While we were representing Jeremy, Alex re-retained my firm to assist him with some post-dissolution of marriage issues. It was at this time that I learned that Rita was Alex's ex-wife, Jeremy's pregnant fiancée. When Alex revealed this, I immediately contacted the Florida Bar Ethics Hotline to determine whether a conflict of interest existed. They confirmed that there was none, yet.

However, matters quickly unraveled. Alex's post-dissolution problems were in large part due to Rita's relationship with Jeremy, especially considering Alex was now dating Jeremy's wife, Renee. Are you following this? Not surprisingly, the Lubsens and their lovers eventually ended up eating dinner at the same restaurant, and the situation was ripe for disaster. Jeremy and Alex entered into a physical altercation, creating a clear conflict of interest between Jeremy and myself. I immediately moved to withdraw from my representation of this "problem child" client, and was relieved to wish him the best of luck with new counsel. He, on the other hand, had to spend some extra money on legal fees getting his new lawyer "up to speed." He would not have had to do so had he been honest with me from the beginning; I would have referred him to another lawyer from the get-go.

CHAPTER FIVE
What Makes an Effective Collaborative Attorney?

An effective collaborative attorney is confident in her ability to practice law and has an appropriate amount of experience in her practice area, in this case in the dissolution of marriage context. As in any other practice method or area, it is crucial for your attorney to be skilled and knowledgeable of the substantive law pertaining to the subject matter. Your attorney should instill confidence based on her experience.

Your lawyer should also be well-versed in how to participate appropriately in the collaborative process. She must have made the "paradigm shift," from litigation to collaboration, successfully. The best way for her to ensure this is to have attended at least one collaborative basic training and to have at least observed, if not participated actively in at least one collaborative divorce. She should also be an active member of a collaborative practice group.

An effective collaborative attorney is open-minded and settlement-driven, yet unwilling to force an improper settlement just to close the case. Your attorney should listen to your concerns, *hear* them, understand them, and help you to reach a settlement that meets your most compelling interests. You won't be thrilled with every aspect of your agreement, but, if your most important goals are met as well as possible, you'll be more likely to view the settlement positively and to abide by it.

An effective collaborative attorney is an active listener who appreciates when to listen quietly while others express their feelings. Many traditional litigators have difficulty doing this because it is generally *not* a valuable skill during the trial process. Often, in litigation, the attorney who argues the loudest or the longest is the one who wins. But a good collaborative lawyer understands that, in working to reaching a settlement that meets both participants' interests, it's important to listen to what those interests are, and to hear and understand them.

An effective collaborative attorney understands the difference between a position and an interest and knows to listen carefully and actively for underlying interests. Such an attorney will work hard to help the facilitator uncover the fundamental concerns at play in her client's case, for both her client and her client's spouse. She will ask the difficult questions and facilitate the intellectual shift in thinking that takes place when a client comprehends the difference between his position and his true interest.

Such an attorney will demonstrate basic brainstorming, option-building, problem-solving, and consensus constructing skills for her client and his spouse. She will work collaboratively with the rest of the team to model these abilities that the couple must master in order to effectively co-parent going forward, if there are children (of any age) of the marriage.

She and the other attorney on the team, the lawyer representing her client's spouse, will also demonstrate and teach both parents the communication skills in which they will be required to engage to avoid conflict in their post-divorce future lives.

An effective collaborative attorney refrains from forcing her own notions about what worked in other cases on the participants. An attorney who turns everything into a fight or is opportunistically adversarial cannot successfully collaborate. To be an effective collaborative advocate requires more than being adversarial; a collaborative attorney understands that concept and does not bully her preconceived ideas onto the spouses.

An effective collaborative attorney allows other team members to shine and appreciates the different skills that each one brings to the table. This attorney understands the benefits of working with other professionals, so that both clients receive the benefit of all of the professionals' strengths. Truly collaborative attorneys will be able to give you examples of how their previous clients have benefited from these specialized professionals, and how their collaborative divorces generally proceeded more smoothly as a result.

Working on a collaborative divorce team is very gratifying. It's always more beneficial to work with colleagues toward common goals without the pressure of trying to gain the upper hand (which is what litigation is all about). Many collaborative professionals work together often (given how small our communities are), another benefit because the professionals enjoy a camaraderie that will assuredly grease the wheels of peaceful negotiations.

An effective collaborative attorney understands the advantages of using the collaborative process. She understands that when spouses reach an agreement together, they are more likely to abide by it and to suffer less conflict down the road. Additionally, people who treat each other well during the process will be better equipped to maintain positive relationships with one another once the divorce is over. Your collaborative attorney, like you, should understand that your future relationships with your soon-to-be-ex spouse and your children are important assets, just as are the financial ones.

An effective collaborative attorney is compassionate to every member of the team. Your attorney's job is to protect your interests in a fair way while also working with the team to satisfy your spouse's interests. The result is that, on occasion, you may feel that your attorney is being overly considerate of your spouse's concerns. But agreeing to work collaboratively at the beginning of the process requires each party both to respect the other's concerns and interests, and also to understand that an agreement cannot be signed until each of their goals are met.

An effective collaborative attorney must be open to the process and understand that there may be a better, less damaging way for couples to divorce than litigation. A collaborative attorney should be able to negotiate without giving in, and to appreciate the benefit of negotiations based on integrity, honor, and support.

It's a funny thing about collaborative cases; trial lawyers are so accustomed to our secret language that it turns out that collaborative practice not only calls for making the paradigm shift in our attitudes, but it also requires making that adjustment in the very language we use when we discuss our cases. The special shorthand that my staff and I use, in which the opposing counsel is "OC" and an opposing party is "OP," no longer seems appropriate or even accurate in our collaborative cases. Now the other client's attorney is no longer an "opposing" lawyer; she is a member of the same collaborative team, a teammate. It is tempting to call her "co-counsel" (although that would be confusing for the trial bar, where "co-counsels" are traditionally the two or more lawyers retained by the same client to work toward the same goal[5]). Together, we are working diligently and cooperatively towards the same goal as both of our clients, creating an agreement that maximizes the goals and interests of them both.

---

[5] According to Miriam-Webster, co-counsel is an attorney who assists in or shares the responsibility of representing one client.

Quiz — Is Your Lawyer Truly Collaborative?

Use this quiz to determine whether your lawyer is a true collaborative lawyer:

1. Does he cringe at the idea of being considered a bulldog attorney? Does he wince when someone asks for a pit bull lawyer? Does he look away when someone calls for a "Rambo" lawyer?

2. Is he a team player (as opposed to a cowboy)?

3. Does he believe that divorcing spouses can and should treat each other amicably and respectfully? Can he help teach them to do that?

4. Can he explain the benefits of interest-based negotiations? Does he understand how that differs from positional bargaining?

5. Is he a problem solver? Can he teach problem solving techniques to his collaborative clients?

6. Does he consider that it's important for divorcing parents to maintain a civil relationship with one another, even after the dissolution of their marriage?

7. Does he communicate well? Can he model good communication skills with the rest of his collaborative team for the divorcing spouses' benefit?

8. Does he think that both a husband and a wife should feel that they have won in their divorce?

9. Can he explain and does he appreciate the strengths that neutral professionals bring to the collaborative team setting?

10. Is he a member of the International Academy of Collaborative Professionals? Has he joined a collaborative practice group? Can he tell you if there are any such groups in your area?

11. Does he believe that the collaborative process is the best option for families for whom divorce is inevitable?

12. If he were getting divorced, would he choose CP for his family?

If you answer "yes" to 0-4 of these questions, then your lawyer is a litigator, and not a collaborative attorney.

If you answer "yes" to 5-8 of these questions, then your lawyer might be a collaborative lawyer, and you might be successful with him representing you in that process.

If you answer "yes" to 9-12 of these questions, then your lawyer is a collaborative attorney, and you have a high probability of concluding that process successfully with him. Not only that, you will learn some serious problem solving skills, as well as how to communicate effectively in the process. Congratulations!

A Good Trial Attorney is Not Always a Good Team Player

I often represent lawyers in their divorces, sometimes without the spouse being aware that I am there, advising the lawyer spouse. But however I participate, my clients are savvy enough to know that they don't want to be in court as a party. Here is one such client's saga.

The "Opposition"

We married young. My wife saw me through law school and stayed home for the next thirty-eight years. During that time, we had four boys and raised them well. With my satisfying and successful career, I couldn't see myself ever retiring. Although work required that I travel quite a bit, I still managed to make time for my boys when I was in town. I participated in the federal, state, and local bar associations, was a member of my local inn of court, and was active in Rotary Club.

One day my boys were grown and having children of their own. The day my youngest turned thirty, I came home and my wife said she wanted a divorce. I was sixty-five. "Lynn, what are you saying?"

"I don't love you anymore, Rick. I don't want to live with you and I want to sever our relationship." It was apparent she had been contemplating this for some time.

"Why?" I asked, stupidly.

She responded quickly. "Because we don't share a life. I've been your maid for any number of years now. The boys are grown and there's no reason for us to stay together anymore. It's time that I waited on myself." Her face was red, her anger palpable.

"I've spent thirty-eight years supporting you, creating a life for both of us to enjoy. And it's only now that the boys are grown that we can enjoy the fruits of my labor." I was totally perplexed, and becoming a little angry. "Can we discuss this with your therapist?" I hoped that her counselor might be able to fix this. Little did I know.

She agreed to meet with her LMHC, a licensed mental health counselor she had been seeing for the last five years. Heidi was a lovely girl, and had helped us through a couple of rough spots when we had been unable to smooth them out for ourselves. I didn't discount her abilities. But when we went, it was clear that they had already discussed Lynn's plans to part from me. There was nothing that I could do to prevent it.

As a trial lawyer, I've never practiced family law, but have plenty of friends who do. I'd heard horror stories about how families destroyed themselves in the litigation arena. But I had also heard of a new way to approach the divorce process. It made a way to negotiate a marital settlement agreement that a court could then simply rubber-stamp, without interfering with a couple's ability to make decisions about how to divide their assets and parent their children. More importantly, our personal business and finances would remain private, instead of being broadcast all over the courthouse. I decided that this might be a better route to take, and did my homework.

I found several attorneys in the area who were collaboratively-trained. Their websites appeared more welcoming and approachable than those of family law litigators. One site really spoke to me. Joryn Jenkins' firm was called *Open Palm Law* because "an open palm holds more sand than a closed fist." As I perused the website, I noticed that the attorneys and staff were smiling serenely. Their profiles gave me a sense of what type of people they were, not just what type of attorneys. Even the website colors were soothing. It included a picture of Joryn holding her little white dog. I was immediately drawn to this firm.

Strangely, I had heard of Joryn years before as a dynamic trial attorney. I had seen her on many occasions at bar events, as well as teaching seminars on ethics and mediation, and she had struck me always as a high-powered corporate lawyer-type, always dressed for court, in a suit and high heels. Her website gave me a different, warmer impression.

When I met with her, I knew almost immediately that she would handle my divorce as compassionately as possible. She was dressed in jeans, flip flops, a casual top, and funky jewelry. Her puppy greeted me at the door, and her office was decorated in a relaxed, Tommy Bahama-style. The soothing fountain immediately relaxed me, and the office smelled of the fresh-baked cookies that were cooling in the kitchen. She greeted me as a fellow member of the bar, which I appreciated, and gave me a tour of her office, showing off her favorite artwork from various Florida photographers.

When we got down to business, and I explained my situation, she listened attentively, nodding her head sympathetically, asking pertinent questions. I could tell that she was truly interested and empathetic to my situation.

While she explained that litigation was an option, she encouraged me towards the collaborative practice method because it was family-focused and less destructive, even arguably *constructive*. If it was important for me to maintain a relationship with my wife after the divorce, collaborative was the best option for achieving that goal. My wife and I had been married for so long that, although we're no longer raising children, she will always be a huge part of my life. We have four boys and six grandchildren, and I expect that more will come. I definitely wanted to maintain as good a relationship as possible with her.

I retained Joryn, and then went home to discuss the collaborative process with my wife. She was skeptical at first, because I was proposing the idea, I suppose, but I encouraged her to discuss the options with a collaboratively-trained attorney of her choosing. She spoke with several litigators and collaborators, and, thankfully, she chose the collaborative alternative.

Once she retained her lawyer, our attorneys worked together to assemble a neutral team facilitator and a neutral financial professional for our team.

I was nervous about the first team meeting, to be held at the financial professional's office. But instead of an intimidating environment, his office, like my attorney's, was warm and welcoming. There was beautiful local artwork on the walls, and large inviting chairs throughout the renovated old home. He had fresh flowers and bowls of candy in most of the rooms. I was immediately at ease.

They were so polite, even my wife's attorney. He was an older guy (What am I saying?! So am I!) with a slow, southern drawl and a bushy mustache. I have never approved of facial hair, and didn't want to like him, but I did anyway. Our team facilitator was a lovely woman, bubbly and energetic. My wife surely noticed that she was wearing the most beautiful snakeskin high heels. The financial professional, a younger, thinner man, wore wire-rimmed spectacles and a bow tie.

The facilitator began by discussing our goals. Mine were to equitably distribute our assets, to help Lynn financially while still maintaining a reasonable amount of income for myself, and to keep a realistic focus during the process. Hers were to fairly divide our assets so that she was financially secure and to find peace with me by the end of the process. I was pleasantly surprised by her second goal. I hadn't realized that she cared to preserve our relationship after the divorce.

We reviewed and signed the participation agreement and began discussing our assets, liabilities, and incomes. The two hours quickly passed and at the end we made appointments for the second full team meeting, as well as for individual meetings with the financial professional to work on our "discovery." That's a lawyer word, by the way, which doesn't really seem to apply in collaborative divorce. We just voluntarily exchanged whatever documents and information we each needed to make decisions during this process. This novel approach for an old seasoned trial attorney like me seemed to work well for us.

By the second meeting, we had exchanged all of our documents. We began to formulate options. Everyone participated in this brainstorming event. We were told there was no idea too odd, too stupid, too impossible to suggest. Every idea was thrown up on the flip chart, with no one credited or criticized for it. By the end of the first hour, we had an amazingly long list of possible outcomes.

Then we started the real work, discussing our interests, or so I thought. When it got down to it, though, Lynn demanded our home and most of the retirement funds, basically all of our assets. On top of that, she seemed stuck on a specific amount of permanent alimony that would give her a higher income than mine while I would be forced to continue working over sixty hours a week indefinitely.

While I loved my job and had no immediate plans to retire, I was getting older, and couldn't work forever. I needed to plan for my eventual retirement, and her proposal would leave me unable to plan accordingly. She basically wanted everything! We talked about all of these "interests" but, no matter what I countered, she was adamant that her way was the only way. I grew discouraged because she was being very positional, not collaborative at all. When the facilitator finally adjourned our meeting, I couldn't wait to get out of there.

I wasn't looking forward to the third meeting. It seemed we weren't making any progress, and our professional fees were quickly mounting. But our facilitator stressed that it was important to keep the process moving forward. There was definitely more tension in the room during the third meeting. I felt like I was at the end of my rope.

Lynn continued with her ridiculous demands. We sat catty-cornered from one another, each across from the other's lawyer. We were getting nowhere, spinning our wheels, wasting time and money. Litigation appeared likely because it seemed it would be impossible for her to negotiate reasonably.

An hour and a half into the meeting, her lawyer put his hand on her shoulder and said with his deep southern twang, "Lynn, I want you to think about what you're saying. Does it really sound reasonable to you?"

I was amazed. I think everyone in the room was thinking the same thing, but I couldn't believe that her attorney was the one to say something. It brought her up short, especially because it came from her own lawyer.

She started to respond and then stopped... and thought. After what seemed like a lifetime, she admitted, "No, I guess not."

The entire mood in the room changed; it was as though everyone had taken a breath of fresh air together. The facilitator complimented Lynn on trying to see it from my point of view and asked her if she would now like to consider my offers. She agreed, and we cut the meeting short so that she could privately discuss my various offers with her attorney and the financial professional.

That was the turning point. Our fourth team meeting was our last because we were able to reach a very reasonable agreement. She got the house, and I received more of the retirement investments to make up for it. She agreed to a fair amount of permanent alimony.

We are still friends. We can both visit with our grandkids

without worrying about whether the other will be there at the same time. It's fine if they are.

She eventually decided to sell the house which was too big for one person or even for two. Last month she went to Costa Rica for vacation. She asked me to continue her garage sale (she'd had one the weekend before she left) to sell the rest of her furniture, after she'd moved out of the house and put it on the market. I was happy to help her.

Here's the thing. I'm a trial attorney. I've never done anything different, although I remember when mediation made its big coming out and everyone was skeptical about whether it could be useful. I certainly learned to adapt to that; now the judge in every case I have sends us to mediation at some point. I think collaborative divorce is like that, but even more so. If divorce is inevitable, why would anyone go to court, which is so destructive, to get divorced, when they can use this kinder, gentler method of restructuring their family relationships, which is so constructive?

Reconstruction, Not Destruction

CHAPTER SIX
The Collaborative Problem Solving Road Map

The collaborative team guides the clients to work together to solve their problems. To solveany problem efficiently, they must follow these steps:

Step 1: Establish the ground rules. They are:
- Be polite, patient, and honest.
- Listen actively without interrupting the speaker.
- Focus on the future and avoid unnecessary discussions of the past. Focus on resolving conflict and avoid assessing blame.
- Speak only for yourself, using "I" instead of "You" sentences. "You" statements place blame on the other party and do not allow the statement-maker to admit to any culpability. The other person will resent the speaker for those comments; thus they hinder negotiations. Alternatively, using "I" statements opens the discussion for exploration, creativity, and changes in response to the situation. "I" sentences allow for a review of an individual's own responses to the situation that exists.

Step 2: Identify and prioritize your interests and concerns.

Understanding the difference between a position and a goal or interest is an important step in effective problem-solving. Focusing on positions, rather than on interests, limits settlement options, and sometimes results in agreements that fail to satisfy the participants' true interests.

In the collaborative process, the professional team works to focus the participants on achieving their goals, rather than on demanding satisfaction of their positions. This enables each one to identify and to define his or her goals. Then the team helps generate multiple settlement options to accomplish them. Identifying goals expands bargaining room and helps spouses understand that there is more than one way to resolve the issues of their divorce. Once identified, they can prioritize their most important goals, which then allows them to comfortably consider compromising on their less important objectives.

In addition, clear identification of big-picture goals at the outset helps them see that they share many common interests and concerns, which will play an important role in achieving the best possible outcome.

Step 3: Address any temporary issues either you or your spouse may have.

Certain temporary concerns must be tackled first because clients will not be able to effectively negotiate if they are fixated on urgent issues that they feel must be addressed *now*. It's difficult to focus on a permanent timesharing schedule when you don't know how you are going to pay your late electrical bill.

Step 4: Gather and exchange your information.

Before you can reach a full settlement agreement, collect all of the necessary information. Initially in CP, clients exchange financial and other important material. Then they review and evaluate it with the appropriate neutral professional(s), and sometimes with their own counsel, as well, so that, when they come to the conference table to negotiate with the full team there, they are fully aware and prepared for those discussions.

Step 5: Brainstorm your options.

Brainstorming provides an open environment in which the entire team participates. The participants should feel as though their thoughts and opinions are being heard. The team will listen actively when brainstorming, but the process will have a relaxed and casual feel.

Brainstorming should be fast-paced so that clients don't have time to self-evaluate or to arrive at preconceptions about options. No idea is a bad idea. Each person at the table should be encouraged to think outside the box, and discouraged from criticizing each other's ideas. Even what might be evaluated as "ridiculous," or "ludicrous," or even impossible suggestions are acceptable because they sometimes lead to other more helpful ideas.

Additionally, the team will avoid rewarding ideas because participants may focus on those suggestions and close their minds to alternatives. Judgment and analysis at this stage stunts contributions and limits creativity. By exploring as many proposals as possible, clients gain the best chance of reaching a settlement that addresses their most important interests.[6]

Step 6: Evaluate your options.

After thorough brainstorming, the team members will weigh, tweak, and trade options as they work to reach a final settlement. This is when the team, or perhaps an individual lawyer, will discuss the ideas of BATNA (the best alternative to a negotiated agreement) and WATNA (the worst alternative to a negotiated agreement). At this point, the clients will evaluate how well their interests can be met by the proposed solutions. The team will discuss the cost and benefit of each proposal to each spouse. The team will ask each client to step into the other client's shoes and analyze whether he or she would be happy with the proposal if he or she was on the other side.

Step 7: Select your best available options.

After creatively brainstorming and evaluating the clients' options, it is time for them to decide. No one forces a decision. It is their process, and, ultimately, they are the ones who have to deal with the decisions that they will make.

---

[6] For more on brainstorming, see Chapter Nine, page 145.

You have all heard of a "marriage of convenience?" This is a term that originated in medieval times. It refers to a marriage contracted for motives other than the reasons of relationship, family, or love. Instead, such a marriage is orchestrated for personal gain or some other sort of strategic purpose, such as for political advancement.

The Thank-You Note

I once worked on what one might call a "divorce of convenience." Beebee Salerno had phoned me, out of the blue, to ask if I would handle her divorce collaboratively. She explained that she had heard me on the radio, discussing my participation in Florida's first *pro bono* collaborative divorce and why I believed so strongly in this means for resolving the issues that arise when people want to dissolve their marriages, and she knew right away that that's what she and her husband wanted.

Well, this explanation sounded a bit odd, so I asked her some background questions. Beebee informed me that she was 76 years old and had been happily married (for the second time) for 26 years. Sal, her 78-year-old husband, had recently been diagnosed as suffering from early stage Alzheimer's disease, and they were both concerned that she would not be able to care for him once his illness became acute. Nor could they afford the help that such care would require. She informed me that, in their hearts, they did not want to be divorced. However, given their understanding of the law regarding Medicare and Social Security, and what they had been led to believe by their friends and Sal's doctor, they would be better off if her premarital assets (a trailer and the land it sat on) were not called into play when the time came to seek government aid.

I should probably also mention that, between the two of them, they had seven children, although none together, and all adults.

She had heard me on the radio, had researched me on-line, and had gone on to investigate collaborative practice. Thus, she was already well-informed about the positive aspects of the collaborative process, and was under the impression that I could help both her and her husband achieve this new status in their relationship, without costing them an arm and a leg, and without alienating either one from the other.

When she arrived for the consultation, he came with her. They walked into my conference room holding hands and smiling, two small, somewhat shrunken old people, their eyes twinkling in a mass of wrinkles. They looked curiously alike, and had obviously dressed up for the appointment. "We do everything together, except when he goes to work." (He bagged groceries at the local supermarket.) Still, I met with her alone, while he waited in the reception area.

My chief concern initially was that their marriage was not "irretrievably broken," as required under Florida law. When I explained my apprehension, she convinced me that, under their circumstances, their desire to terminate the marriage, for whatever reason, satisfied the "irretrievably broken" legal standard.

I gave her the list of lawyers who had been collaboratively trained in my community and, in short order, received a phone call from one with whom I'd worked before, informing me that he had been retained by the husband. We agreed on a process facilitator and a neutral financial professional, and scheduled our first team meeting.

One would think that this collaboration was a no-brainer. One would be wrong. CP is comprised of meetings between the clients and each professional, sometimes separately and sometimes together, usually called off-line meetings, as well as full team meetings of all the professionals and the two clients. As the process here revved up, after everyone signed the collaborative participation agreement at our first full team meeting, I became concerned by some of Beebee's seemingly innocuous comments in our first off-line meeting together (while Sal waited in the lobby). It occurred to me that my client might be setting him up so that she could legally discard responsibility for him when he became too "difficult."

As it turned out, at the same time, my collaborative team-mate (the lawyer representing Mr. Salerno) began to suspect that Sal might fully intend to leave Beebee as soon as the divorce became final, that he might really *want* to be divorced, a fact of which, if true, she was not aware.

Transparency is critical to the collaborative process. My teammate and I therefore discussed off-line with the other professionals (especially with our facilitator) our concerns that the clients might not have been straightforward with each other about their reasons for seeking a divorce. We agreed to take a wait-and-see approach, understanding that we would broach the issues before too much time passed if our suspicions became more serious. This was primarily because the facilitator had not picked up on the same vibes, and she had also spent considerable time with the couple, both separately and together.

It is just as well that we took that approach. In our second full team meeting, we discussed with both Salernos the fact that they had no wills. Thus, when they divorced, and one of them died, the other would not automatically become heir to at least a major portion of the deceased spouse's estate, as he or she would, by law, if the surviving spouse. And the fact that they each had children not related to the other made this cause for concern.

At the very next full team meeting, the couple asked if it would be possible to involve a collaboratively trained probate lawyer. It was. Sal and Beebee then clarified that they each wanted to ensure that the other inherited his or her entire estate in the event that he or she predeceased the other. As this discussion developed, it became clear from the interactions between them, and especially their affectionate body language, that our concerns about transparency had not been justified.

This conclusion was borne out over several meetings, both full team and off-line. In retrospect, I have to believe that both my teammate and I had met with these clients at one point after they had had a disagreement or some sort of spat, which is normal in any marriage, and which had blown over as they so often do. In any event, it has now been many months since the participants signed their marital settlement agreement, the court entered its final judgment of dissolution of marriage, and the clients executed their estate planning documents, leaving everything that they own to each other. I recently received a thank-you note, signed by both of them:

We had to do something so very hard and emotionally very upsetting. But we knew we had to do a divorce because of our situation. We want you and everyone on the team to know that your kindness and each one's expertise will forever be appreciated and remembered. You have all made this difficult journey bearable and possible! Collaborative divorce is a loving way that makes such a task easier, and takes the stress out of it. So to all of you angels we send our heartfelt thanks and love for all you have done for us.

It was signed by both Beebee and Sal, and they delivered it together.

Sometimes, divorce results when one spouse realizes that he or she never really knew the other before they "tied the knot." These are the divorces that prove the old adage "familiarity breeds contempt." It is not uncommon that "a marriage of convenience" becomes a divorce of convenience (for one of them) when this happens.

The Marriage of Convenience

Ivan Ishchenko and Vladimir Kruschev had been best friends back home, in Russia. Both men were large, strapping, quiet types with penetrating blue eyes. Ivan had a lighter disposition, and Vladimir was more serious. Despite the language barrier, it was clear that both men had good, big hearts and romantic spirits. Ivan was an idealist, and his ultimate dream was to enjoy the means to move to America, which he viewed as the land of freedom and opportunity. Vladimir, though a strong man, was content following in Ivan's footsteps — a man whom he not only thought of as a friend, but also as an older brother and mentor.

One day, two American women, friends traveling together on vacation, swept the Russians off their feet, and whisked them back to the United States. Ivan hooked up with Lily, a focused, successful woman with mousy brown hair. Vladimir got involved with Karol, a robust woman with dyed red, frizzy hair. Neither woman had had much luck with dating in the U.S., and they viewed their trip to Russia as an expedition to find husbands. As soon as the women met the two friends in a Russian bar, they vowed to work together to convince them to return to America with them.

And they soon did. After spending just a few weeks together in Russia, the men agreed to travel to America for a month. If all went well, they agreed, they would not return to Russia.

Both men spoke little English, and the ladies spoke no Russian. Nevertheless, before long, they were married. However, while it appears that the language of love was sufficient to forge their unions, it was not strong enough to bind them together forever.

Less than two years into his marriage, Ivan's wife, Lily, filed for divorce. She was a high school teacher, so her income was comparatively small, but she owned several pieces of rental property that she had accumulated during her first divorce. As a result of her habit of investing wisely, by the time of her divorce from Ivan, her net worth was close to one million dollars. Ivan, on the other hand, had been an engineer in his native Russia, but he spoke little English, and could only obtain menial work in the United States, for the nominal rate of ten dollars an hour.

When Lily brought Ivan to the States, she knew that he had no income, assets, or ability to support himself. We took the position that she would have to support him.

In addition to needing her for emotional support and cultural insights, there was a little bit of abuse going on here. Ivan was completely dependent on Lily financially because she grabbed what little he *did* earn and gave him no money to spend. She filed their tax returns and kept the refunds for herself. During their marriage, according to him, she never allowed him to purchase anything for himself. She permitted him to use the Saturn that she had bought for him, but took it away when she filed her petition for divorce. While married, they lived a typical middle class lifestyle, although she was the primary breadwinner and controlled all household purchases.

Because of his low income, his unreliable transportation (he never knew if she would allow him to use the car), and his language and culture barriers, he was vulnerable and needed support. She earned considerably more, had lengthy, stable employment, and supplemented her salary with the rental income. During the short time that they were together, they lived in her home, he drove a car she'd purchased for him, and they both enjoyed a comfortable lifestyle.

Prior to the marriage, Lily had compelled Ivan to sign a prenuptial agreement, which would have left him with nothing in the event that they divorced. We argued that the court should set it aside or recognize that it was void *ab initio*. After all, he'd signed it under duress, without understanding his rights, and without the benefit of an attorney.

Six days prior to their wedding, she had presented him with the agreement. It had been drafted by her attorney. She drove him to *her* friend's home to execute it. The friend purported to translate it and to then also serve as notary.

When Lily handed him the agreement, she said, "You know I

love you Ivan, but I cannot marry you unless you sign this agreement, right here, right now." Although the document was translated into Russian, Ivan was given little time to read it or to consult an attorney about its content or his rights.

A strong desire to make his life and marriage work motivated him. As a transplanted immigrant, Ivan needed Lily both financially and emotionally. He'd left behind his career, his car, his home, his family and his friends — everything he had had in Russia — to be with her. And, it had always been his dream to live in America, though the reality of America did not seem as rosy as he had hoped. Under the circumstances, her threat not to marry him constituted coercion. Without her, he'd be stripped of shelter, a source of income, transportation, or even the means to return to Russia — everything he relied on here. "I sign," he replied quietly in his broken English, pen in hand.

Afterward, she refused to give him a copy of the agreement, eliminating any meaningful opportunity to review it with an attorney. We later discovered, when we *did* obtain a copy, that the agreement itself misrepresented Ivan's income by stating that he earned $36,000 annually when he actually had no income at all at the time. Additionally, it had been notarized by a friend of Lily, without witnesses.

We requested that Ivan receive a special equity in their marital assets because she had constrained him to relinquish all of his earnings during their marriage to her and given him nothing in return to spend. Despite the brevity of their two-year marriage, we requested alimony based on her superior financial position and his vulnerability.

Soon after Lily petitioned to divorce Ivan, her best friend, Karol, followed suit and filed against Vladimir. During their marriage, he had served as primary caregiver for both the child they conceived shortly after their marriage, as well as of the toddler Karol had adopted shortly before her trip to Russia.

Shortly after filing, Karol unilaterally sold their home, accepted a new job, and bought a house in Kansas City. "Vladimir, I am moving and taking the children with me. I do not want you to follow me." Vladimir felt so betrayed and alone, and he was concerned that Karol would be able to proceed as she threatened, and he would never see his son again. Because a standing order prohibits this type of behavior while a divorce is pending, we filed a motion to prevent her from relocating.

Like his friend, Ivan, Vladimir had executed a prenuptial agreement under duress, without understanding his rights, and without the benefit of an attorney. Their situations paralleled one another: minimal English, low income, no assets, and an inability to earn a living. Like his friend, Ivan, Vladimir worked a job that only paid ten dollars an hour; his, however, was part-time.

During their marriage, Karol had been the primary breadwinner. She was a senior vice president at a local bank, earning well over $250,000/year. In addition, she was worth well over a million bucks. During their marriage, Vladimir supported her career by taking care of the house and also of both of their children. Therefore, we requested that Vladimir's prenuptial agreement also be set aside, and that he receive alimony and primary residential responsibility of the child they shared.

Then Karol assaulted Vladimir. (They were still living together at the time.) He was awarded a temporary injunction for protection against domestic violence. However, as unfair as this may sound, the judge allowed Karol to remain in the marital home, because it was in her name alone, having been purchased before the two were married. Joshua, her adopted son, remained with her, as Vladimir had never been offered the opportunity to adopt him. Vladimir and Dmitri were forced to move in with Ivan into his tiny apartment.

Every week, Karol spent Monday through Friday in Kansas City at her new job. During her travels, she left her adopted child, Joshua (who had only known Vladimir as a primary caregiver for the three years prior to the domestic violence incident), at home with a domestic who spoke only Spanish and had no special childcare training.

Because he was a large man with the severe temperament common to Russians, we knew that obtaining a permanent injunction would be an uphill battle (although Karol was fairly brutish, as well). While the courts are supposed to be gender-neutral, there is no doubt that it is more difficult to obtain an injunction for a man against a woman.

The judge was not amused when Vladimir answered a question with a simple "Neh," and the interpreter "translated" the response as a lengthy diatribe. After several "translations," the judge angrily removed the interpreter from the courtroom. After the hearing, which we lost, the two ranted at me in Russian all the way from the courthouse to my vehicle. Although I had no clue what they were saying, there are few angrier-sounding languages than Russian, so they made their point!

Ultimately, we were able to settle the Russians' cases. Vladimir's case was far easier to resolve; once she was over her initial anger at being thwarted in her plans, Karol was not so insensitive as to fail to realize that both of her children cherished their relationships with Vladimir, their father and stepfather respectively, and the only Dad either of them had ever known. We were eventually able to forge an agreement, using the services of a talented mediator, in which Karol supported Vladimir's move to Kansas City and helped him find better employment, and Vladimir remained as part-time caregiver for the children.

Ivan was not so lucky. Lily refused to admit that she had taken advantage of his status, and there were no children involved to soften her heart. Furthermore, we were unable to get the judge to award Ivan even the smallest temporary attorney's fees, so we were working for free (involuntarily) from the get-go. With our coaching, Ivan eventually was able to approach Lily directly. He convinced her to fund his trip back to Russia, but she refused to do any more than that. We never heard from him again and can only hope that his old friends were able to help him get back on his feet once he returned to his homeland.

Judges Decide Based on a Snapshot of People's Lives

Quiz — *Is Collaborative Divorce the Option For You?*

Take this quiz to find out if the collaborative option is right for you:

1.   Do you want a judge who doesn't know you or your kids, or share your values, to decide how you live the rest of your life?

2.   Do you want your kids to be put in the middle of your divorce, carrying messages (and tales) between you and your soon-to-be ex?

3.   Do you want to have to file for bankruptcy protection as soon as you obtain your divorce?

4.   Do you want to spend years in limbo, waiting to get your divorce heard by a judge?

5.   Even after your trial, do you want to spend months waiting for a judge to decide how you will live the rest of your life?

6.   Do you want to spend your life's savings, and your parents' retirement funds, fighting your soon-to-be ex-spouse in court?

7.   Do you want to force your friends to choose sides in a war with your soon-to-be ex?

8.   Do you want to be compelled to ask a judge's permission before you can take your kids on a vacation?

9.   Do you want to be forced to ask someone you don't know and who doesn't know you or your kids, or share your values, for permission to relocate more than 50 miles from your current residence?

10. Do you want every decision you make until your kids are 18 years old to be an exhausting hassle?

If you answered "no" to 0-3 of these questions, then you are an unlikely candidate for a collaborative divorce and the traditional courtroom route is recommended for you.

If you answered "no" to 4-6 of these questions, then you are a candidate for a collaborative divorce, and you may be successful in that process.

If you answered "no" to 7-10 of these questions, then you are a prime candidate for CP and have a high probability of concluding that process successfully.

Asking Permission to Take Her Children on Vacation

CHAPTER SEVEN
Beginning the Process

Once the husband and wife retain collaborative attorneys, the collaborative process begins. The attorneys should begin conversations with one another regarding the issues involved in the case and any urgent temporary matters. If a temporary matter must be addressed expeditiously, the lawyers should work quickly to retain the neutral professionals and to schedule the first meeting. If that cannot happen soon enough, the attorneys may need to work together with the participants to resolve the temporary issues before the neutrals are retained.

The lawyers should discuss whether the couple would like to proceed under a one-coach or a two-coach collaborative model. Generally, communities have their own protocols regarding which model is most often used. But certain situations may require a deviation from the standard arrangement. Counsel should be able and willing to modify the venue's typical procedures to meet the specific needs of the participants.

Often, the lawyers will choose a facilitator and a financial neutral with whom one or both has worked successfully in the past. When time is of the essence, or it's likely the two clients cannot agree on which collaborative neutrals to engage, this process works best. But the clients may request that their counsel suggest mental health and financial professionals for the clients to interview before deciding whom to retain. If the participants are more hands-on and reasonable, without time pressures, then permitting them to consult with various neutrals and have a say in who is retained makes good sense. It is the clients' process, and some will want more control over it than others.

Discussions about the need for any other professional neutral, such as a child advocate or an appraiser, will usually occur at this time. However, it may be too early to determine whether those neutrals are necessary.

The attorneys should also discuss the language of the participation agreement. Often standard forms work best, but based on the specific couple involved, the agreement usually used in the community may need to be revised. The attorneys may include their clients in these discussions or may opt to keep them out of this stage of the negotiations. That decision will depend on the clients themselves and how involved and in control of the process they wish to be.

Once the language of the participation agreement has been determined, the attorneys should send it to their clients for their review prior to the first team meeting. If both people have already reviewed the agreement and clarified their questions before the first meeting, less explanation will be required during the full team meeting when all collaborative professionals are billing for their time.

Once the neutrals have been retained, each client will meet with the facilitator to discuss his or her goals, issues, concerns, and the history of the relationship. The facilitator will prepare a report of the interviews for the team so that they have a better understanding of the clients' personalities, their strengths and weaknesses, and how to avoid pitfalls that might arise in the collaborative process based on this personal information.

By now the first professional teleconference and the first full team meeting should be scheduled. The facilitator should prepare the agenda for the team meetings, including agenda items proposed by the clients. These will be e-mailed to the professionals prior to each professional teleconference for discussion, agreement and/or modification, and finalization.

During the teleconference, the professionals will discuss any changes to the agenda, the strategy for each full team meeting (including how best to raise certain sensitive issues), and how to ensure that the process runs smoothly and efficiently. They will brainstorm both on techniques to assist the participants in navigating the collaborative path and on how to share party-to-party communications.

The attorneys will circulate the finalized agenda for each full team meeting to all participants, including their clients, ahead of that meeting. If it isn't the first meeting of the full team, they should include approval of the notes or minutes (different venues use different terminology) from the prior meeting and reports regarding the status of the participants' homework assignments. Relevant documents that will be used during the meeting should be copied and packaged in advance to save time during the meetings.

One of the professionals, or sometimes a "shadow" (a professional who has not yet participated in his first paid collaborative case) will be assigned to take the minutes of the full team meeting to ensure that the team has a record of what occurred. It should be stressed to the clients that, just because something is included in the minutes, it does not mean that it is the participants' agreement.

Within three days of a meeting, the minutes-recorder should remit them to the other professionals, who will then return them with their edits.

Once the professionals have agreed on the minutes, the recorder will send them to the clients, who may also suggest edits. Once the minutes have been finalized, all participants may sign them prior to the next meeting, depending on the protocols established by the team.

The attorneys should meet with their clients prior to each full team meeting. Generally, fifteen minutes immediately beforehand will suffice. The attorneys will likely already have sent the agenda to their clients so that they know what to expect. More than anything, this brief time is important to put them at ease, to answer any questions, to address any concerns, and to prepare them emotionally for the meeting.

It is important to adhere to the agenda during meetings. This routine not only helps to control the clients' anxieties but also, by fulfilling the clients' expectations in this way, this procedure also builds their trust in the collaborative process.

The first team meeting will begin with the facilitator reviewing the clients' goals. The facilitator and other team members will refer to these often throughout the process, reminding the clients of them and anchoring the clients to them, when necessary.

Next, the facilitator should review the protocols or code of conduct[7] with the clients.

---

[7] An example of the participation protocols can be found on the author's website at www.OpenPalmLaw.com.

During the first meeting, the team will review the participation agreement and declaration of principles with the clients, including a discussion of the concepts embodied by the confidentiality, transparency, and disqualification clauses. Some attorneys feel that it is important for the team to read the entire agreement to the participants, asking as they go whether the clients understand and agree. This prevents the clients from claiming later that they didn't understand what they were signing; the team can be confident that they did everything to ensure that they did.

But this practice can be tedious, and the clients tend to become distracted and to fail to really listen. Also, they may become upset and stressed because they are paying all of the professionals for this mind-numbing review. Thus, many attorneys opt to forego the full reading, and instead summarize each section for the clients in a more conversational format, checking often as to whether the clients understand and agree.

Once the reading or review of the participation agreement is complete, the team signs it, and proceeds with the rest of the agenda. It is usually appropriate to next discuss the valuation date for the assets and liabilities. It will also probably be a good time for the clients to schedule appointments with the financial neutral to begin working on their financial document exchange prior to the next joint meeting. The financial professional may help the clients prepare their sworn financial affidavits; in any event, they should be prepared early in the process to identify marital and non-marital assets.

The team should then identify issues, gather relevant information, explore various options, and guide the clients. This will also include a discussion of the clients' immediate concerns.

Early in this process, the team will address the payment of the professionals' fees and any court costs. It is likely that those fees and costs should be paid using marital funds on a monthly basis. A protocol should be set in place early to ensure that this doesn't become a source of regular discussion, irritating to the clients.

Throughout the meeting, the clients may be given "homework" to provide relevant information before the next joint meeting. These tasks must be accomplished within a certain timeframe, often before the next full team meeting. Timely completion reduces the expense to the clients and keeps the process moving forward. Typical homework assignments include the compilation of financial discovery, appraisal of the home, valuation of personal property, research of job opportunities, and work with the child advocate or facilitator towards developing the parenting plan.

In most communities, full team meetings are set for only two hours, and the team works hard to accomplish their agenda items during that period. After two hours, people tend to lose focus, and may become more emotional. However, in some situations — such as when the divorce must happen quickly or the participants are often unavailable — if both clients agree, then the meetings can be scheduled to last longer.

Prior to adjourning, if this has not already been accomplished, the team should schedule the next professional teleconference *and* the next full team meeting. All team members are encouraged never to cancel and to be on time to avoid unnecessary delay and aggravation.

After each meeting, the attorneys should again meet briefly with their clients to get feedback and to address any of the clients' concerns. Each attorney should answer his client's questions, and ensure that his client understands what occurred during the meeting and his or her homework, and that the client is comfortable with how the process is proceeding.

Then the professionals will meet again to briefly debrief. The professionals constructively critique and complement one another so that the individual team members can learn what was effective and what may have been damaging to the process in this unique divorce. The facilitator offers specific insights into what took place, what worked and what did not. The professionals address any concerns and make suggestions to improve the next meeting.

Thereafter, the process continues as explained above until the clients have reached their full settlement.[8]

---

[8] For a timeline of a typical collaborative case, go to the author's website at www.OpenPalmLaw.com.

The Full Team Meets

The Apology

My name is Sean. Katie and I were married when she was twenty and I was twenty-four. I was very much in love with her back then. But that was nineteen years ago.

Over the last few years, we've grown apart. We'd been married for 17 years when I finally began to realize what had slowly been eating away at our love. Katie had gotten her college degree early in our marriage, and I had asked her often to get to work on her career. We had never had children, but she seemed content to work as a part-time bookkeeper. Over time it seemed that *she* had become my child.

Whenever I broached the topic, Katie seemed afraid of full-time employment. With very few friends, she relied entirely on me for her emotional well-being, as well as financial support. But that's not what I had signed on for so many years ago; I always thought, and still do, that marriage should be a partnership.

I didn't give up easily. We tried marriage counseling for over a year. But early in our relationship, she had gotten stuck in a holding pattern. While I had matured and broadened my interests, she had remained in her own little rut. Ironically, the counseling enabled me to understand that I no longer loved her in a romantic way, but only as a sibling might, or a parent, or, at best, a friend.

Don't get me wrong; I had many happy memories, but I was increasingly frustrated by her inability to grow up. The more I tried to explain what I wanted out of our marriage, the more she withdrew into her shell.

When I finally suggested a "trial separation," I was done, I wanted a divorce. But I couldn't say it to her face. We needed some distance between us. She needed to prove to herself she could survive on her own. At least that's what I hoped for.

I continued to pay all the expenses of both homes. As a meticulous and methodical person, I had always handled the money. I paid all the bills at the end of every month; there was never a balance on our credit cards. We never got in over our heads. On our fifteenth anniversary, I paid off the mortgage on our tidy, quaint home. I contributed to our retirement plans every month. While neither rich, nor even well-to-do, we were comfortable.

When we agreed (and I use that term loosely; Katie wasn't happy about it) to separate, I rented a one-bedroom apartment not far from our house. I knew she'd feel safer if she stayed in the marital home and I didn't want to upset her more than necessary.

Over the next few months, I deposited money in the joint account so she could pay her expenses—taxes, insurance, utilities, and so on. I continued to pay both of our credit cards.

May 2013, two months into our separation, I summoned the courage to tell her I wanted a divorce. I had consulted several divorce attorneys and I thought I knew my choices. One, we could do the kitchen-table divorce, hashing out our agreement ourselves while sitting in our own kitchen. Two, we could go to a mediator, a lawyer or other professional trained in family law and mediation, to work through our disagreements. Three, we could go to war, fighting it out in divorce court.

I hoped to empower Katie, to help her to accept and agree to a simple, inexpensive dissolution of our marriage. We had no children; we had no debt. Although I was the main breadwinner over the years, it seemed fair to split our assets half and half. The lawyers I'd consulted agreed about one thing; if I wanted a divorce, she couldn't stop it, but she could drag her feet, slowing it down and costing much more money.

I called her. "We need to talk." We arranged a time for me to stop by the house.

When I arrived, she suggested we go sit in the kitchen with a cup of coffee. Walking through the house was a little unnerving. Nothing had changed since I'd left ten weeks before. (I had taken nothing but my clothes.) All of my family photos were still clustered on the mantelpiece. My trophies, knick knacks, and magazines were exactly as I had left them. It was a *museum*.

Although the coffee was already made, she seemed flustered so I asked if she could make me a cup of tea. Giving her something to do might calm her down. After much banging around in the dish cupboards and the microwave, she finally set a steaming cup of tea in front of me and sat across from me at the table. I drew a deep breath and plunged in, before I could lose my nerve.

"Katie, this isn't working. It's time. I want a divorce."

She was silent. Her eyes puddled. Finally, she spoke. "How can you say that?" Tears pooled on her lower lids and quivered there. Then they spilled out and chased one after the other, down either side of her face. Each drop was quickly followed by another.

I reminded her gently of the marriage counselor's advice. "Katie, I've always loved you. I always will. But we've grown apart. We fight all the time. We just don't have anything in common anymore. I feel like we can still be friends, but I'm just not in love with you anymore." I hated that I sounded like I was whining so I stopped . . . and waited.

She dug her fingers into her hair and started pulling at it. It was still short, the same pageboy style as the day we were married. But now grey strands mingled with the dark brown hair, despite the fact she was only thirty-nine. (Who am I to talk? Mine went grey and I'm completely bald on top, so I keep my entire head bare.) Her cheeks turned red, a sign she was about to cry. Sure enough, a sob forced its way out. She placed her head down on the table, resting it on her crossed forearms, her chest heaving, and hid her face.

"What am I going to do?" She hiccupped, sobbing uncontrollably.

I took the box of tissues from the counter and placed it next to her on the table. I knew this woman. There would be no conversation today. "We'll talk when you're calmer." I kissed her on the cheek and left.

Over the next few months, I encouraged her to retain a lawyer, but nothing I said made a difference. She refused to even talk to one, not in words, but by her inaction. When I considered my choices, I didn't like any of them. I needed better counsel, so I looked for another attorney.

I finally found someone who told me about collaborative divorce. It sounded better than anything else I'd considered. It would cost less than traditional courtroom divorce. It should take less time, and, God knew, I'd already invested more than was fair to get this done. The stress should be less. Because it would involve a mental health practitioner, it should provide a safe environment for Katie to come to grips with her freedom from me. And it should ensure that our personal, confidential information would remain private. I hoped she would agree to it.

For months Katie had refused to respond to my lawyer's written entreaties to consult a collaborative attorney. I finally told my lawyer, Joryn, to go ahead and file suit, but to continue to reach out to her with the offer to collaborate. But it wasn't until I withdrew all the money from the joint account that she finally did.

The attorneys had agreed to Katie's request that she and I would choose the two neutral members of the team, the mental health facilitator and the financial, rather than the lawyers, as they sometimes do. Katie and I had separately interviewed all of the professionals Joryn and Aaron had jointly proposed, and I had agreed to Katie's selections. None of the choices were either unacceptable or far superior to the rest, so it provided another way to empower her in the process.

Joryn had prepped me for the first collaborative meeting. I assume Aaron had prepped Katie, as well. I had met with Alicia, the facilitator, and Rob, the financial neutral, ahead of time. Katie had, as well. Joryn explained that the lawyers had received the neutrals' reports so that they were better prepared for the meeting. After we concluded this process, I discovered what Alicia had conveyed to our team, but I will share it now. About Katie, she had said:

> Katie has not thought about personal property she may want and has not completed the financial affidavit. She feels she may need to sell the marital home but has not considered or explored alternative living options. These facts tell me she has been emotionally paralyzed this past year and that avoidance and compartmentalization are her coping mechanisms.
>
> Katie believes that the power structure in the marriage was inequitable and she fears that this dynamic may play out in our process. She fears Sean will take advantage of her and she needs lots of

reassurance here. "He always got his way and I allowed it." She was teary throughout my interview and will likely be emotional during our process, something she feels Sean is uncomfortable with.

About me, she said:

> Sean admits that he is impatient and that he is frustrated by Katie's lack of motivation in her career and lack of movement regarding the divorce. He believes that Katie is resentful that he did not continue in marriage counseling but he was unhappy and needed to move on.

> Sean's focus was on solutions and how we can move quickly and inexpensively. He was kind but has clearly moved on emotionally. He reports that there is one fundamental difference between Katie and him; she believes that he is responsible to care for her for the rest of her life while he believes that he owes her help to get back on her feet. He reports that Katie drags her feet and will avoid making decisions as long as she is allowed to do so. He is concerned that her emotions may play on the team and that they will somehow influence us.

We were an hour into the meeting. We had first reviewed the salient details of the participation agreement which I'd received and read months earlier. I was glad that the team had not spent our valuable time reading it aloud, word for word, especially the part that the unsuccessful termination of the collaborative process would mandate termination of both lawyers' participation in the divorce process. In other words, neither lawyer would be allowed to represent either of us in court.

We had also covered the terms of the team's payment. As I had always paid the bills, I agreed to pay for the professionals throughout the process.

Then we got to the nitty-gritty. How would we deal with the

house? Katie wanted to stay in it, but that wouldn't work unless I paid alimony until she died, which I did *not* want to do.

Surprisingly, Katie spoke up. We had both been relatively silent, simply nodding or "uh-huh"ing to any questions. When Rob raised the issue of the value of the home, Katie glanced around the table and said, "Well, you know, last year Sean asked me to get three quotes from realtors on a good selling price. I got two and they were both in the $260,000 to $300,000 range. I understand that a realtor is always going to estimate high, to assure that we hire him to sell the property, but I *believe* that $260,000 is a good value." She ended her speech with a challenging stare at me.

I suggested quietly. "I don't think it's a waste of money to hire a real estate appraiser. What would it be, $400?"

Aaron agreed. "$350 to $400. Joryn and I can probably pick one for you. Her husband is a commercial real estate appraiser, so even if we don't know of one we've used before in your county, I'm sure he can recommend one."

While Joryn e-mailed her husband on her i-Phone, Rob said, "I can give you a couple of names. What about Kevin Stern or Richard Wallcraft? I've used them in the past and I know they work over there."

Aaron said, "I've never heard of either. Joryn, what do you think?"

She responded, referring to her i-Phone, "My husband says Richard Wallcraft is excellent. He says we should tell him Todd and Rob recommended him." Remembering that Katie had wanted to interview and choose the collaborative neutrals on our team, she inquired, "Katie, is that ok with you?"

Everyone looked at her. She looked mildly surprised to be asked, but affirmed. "Yes, that's great. Can you send me his contact information? I assume I'll have to let him in the house?"

My head was spinning. Was it *really* going to be this easy to reach agreement?

Rob asked "If I send it to you by e-mail, can you print it out?"

Katie's eyes filled with tears again.

"What now?!" I thought.

"No, I can't. The printer isn't working."

Caught off guard, I responded without thinking, "What

happened? Did it break? Why didn't you tell me?"

"It broke last May. You always fixed it and I don't know how. I told you that."

Again, without thinking. "Do you want me to come fix it? That's easy; I'll come fix it."

Sadly, she looked down at the table, slowly shaking her head, quick tears dropping into her lap. Matter-of-factly, Joryn asked "Do you need to print it or can you just read it off your phone?"

Katie looked up. "Yes, I'll do that."

Crisis averted, I sighed. What next?

The next item on the agenda Alicia had sent out beforehand was "Current Expenses/Status Quo." Alicia asked "Are bills getting paid? Are the utilities current? You don't have a mortgage, but what about rent at the apartment? Is the status quo being maintained?"

Again, Katie's eyes overflowed. "I can't pay the bills. Sean took all the money out of the joint account. I've had to go into my savings account just to pay the utilities at the house . . . and the taxes . . . and I even paid the car insurance . . . and not just on my car, but on his, too!"

Okay, great! So now I'm the bad guy. I'd been waiting for this. I tapped Joryn on the shoulder. Speaking softly, I asked "Can we step outside? I need a word with you."

Alicia heard me. "Yes, of course, let's take a break."

Joryn indicated the door behind me. In the hall, she pointed to an empty office. I ducked in there with her hard on my heels. "What's up?" she asked.

"She's doing it. Exactly what I was worried about. She turns on those tears and makes me look like the bad guy to everyone. How do I defend against *that*?"

Joryn put her hand on my shoulder. "Listen to me. You're being overly sensitive. Everyone at that table, except Katie, is a non-judgmental professional. We hear this stuff all day long, every day. If you're concerned about looking like the bad guy, how do you defuse that? Did you empty out the account?"

Although I had not told her, she already knew the answer. "Yes."

"And why did you do that?"

She knew this, too, but I walked her through the explanation. There was a reason she was asking me this. "Because I couldn't get her off the dime. She wasn't responding to me or to you, and she wasn't getting herself an attorney to engage in this process."

"Did it work?"

"Yes."

"Do you have any reason not to replace the money?"

This answer she also knew. "No."

"So go back in there, explain why you did it, and assure her that you'll put the money back." Joryn paused before adding "Can you apologize? Can you tell her, truly, that you're sorry you hurt her feelings?"

Well, *that* was a no-brainer! I nodded.

"Then let's go back in there and you do that." She smiled.

We marched back into the conference room after less than two minutes. Everyone else was still seated.

I began talking before I was actually back in my chair. I looked directly at her. "Katie, I only took the money out because I wanted you to join me in this collaborative process and I couldn't seem to get your attention. I couldn't get you to focus. Now that you're here, I'll put the money back." I hesitated before I added, with emotion, "I'm so sorry I scared you, and I'm truly sorry I hurt your feelings." In the quiet that followed, I added, "I apologize for that."

Dead silence followed. Her eyes were opened very wide.

Then Alicia jumped in, "Well, Sean we really appreciate your apology. I assume that Katie would like the funds put back. Katie?"

Katie nodded, still staring at me. "Sean, how much did you take out?"

I told her.

"When can you put it back?"

"Tonight."

The lawyers, as well as Alicia and Rob, were taking notes. The sounds of Aaron shifting in his seat and clearing his throat seemed unnaturally loud. "Sean, I'd like to thank you for that apology. I know how much Katie appreciates that."

Katie was smiling.

It's never fun to represent the parent accused of sexually abusing a child. One can never be certain whether the accused is guilty of the specified charges, or, indeed, of anything else, in a system in which the other parent's accusation is sometimes a litigation strategy. As the lawyer in that case, all I can be sure of is that that parent is entitled to representation in the judicial process. (But it doesn't always have to be me who serves as that lawyer!)

The Drunk

Pete Peter (can you believe his parents named him that?) entered my office, his lanky frame draped in baggy, grass-stained clothing and his dirty, sweaty face crowned by scruffy, auburn hair. The creases enveloping his eyes made him seem older than thirty-seven. His slow speech, unlike a southern drawl, sounded like he was either confused or thinking hard about his next words. Despite the fact that his girlfriend had scheduled the consult, and accompanied him, his blue-eyed stare stripped me visually, triggering invisible waves of violation. After his intrusive look, his lips lifted in a smirk.

The story he told was unusual. He slowly began without looking me in the eyes, "Two years ago, I was charged with sexual battery on Natalie, my wife's twelve-year-old daughter from a boyfriend before me." He looked up and into my eyes, pleading, "I swear, I didn't mean to do anything wrong. I just don't know what happened. I got home late from drinking with my buddies. I was really drunk. Like, I have no recollection of how I even got home. I think I watched some TV because there was an open bag of chips and a can of Coke sitting by the television in the morning. I must have gone to my room and stripped because that is where I found my clothing in the morning. I think I passed out in me and my wife's bed. She was working the night shift as a nurse at the local hospital."

He nervously fumbled with a candy wrapper that he had in his hand and continued. "I woke up the next morning, but I was in Natalie's bed, naked. I was so confused. I didn't understand how I had gotten there. Natalie claimed that I had crawled naked into her bed with her in the middle of the night. I don't know why she didn't wake me up and tell me to get out. Or scream." He looked down again and said quietly, "She also told her mother that I had touched her 'private areas.' I would never do that knowingly. I must have thought I was in bed with my wife."

I tried not to look too shocked and disgusted. But I was flabbergasted as to how this could happen. Even if his version of the story was correct, how could he have become so intoxicated? And I didn't want to think about the fact that he might be lying. "So what happened with that case," I asked.

"Well, I agreed to the court's entry of an injunction, putting me out of my home. When I then pleaded guilty to felony child abuse and domestic violence, the judge prohibited me from having any contact with any of the children, not just Natalie, but also the two I share with my wife. Because it was my first offense, I was sentenced to five years of probation." I suppose it was admirable that he did not want to subject Natalie to a full hearing, with the concomitant police investigation and the inevitably painful and grueling cross examination.

Following the events of that night, Pete joined Alcoholics Anonymous and, as far as I knew, stopped drinking. Nevertheless, during our representation of Pete, I repeatedly wondered whether he was a pervert . . . or just a drunk. I continued to weigh the two options . . . pervert or drunk? Drunk or pervert? Call me gullible, but ultimately I concluded that he was just a drunk.

As a result of his guilty plea, Pete lost his job as a radiologist and was forced to find another. Because he had paid for college by working for a landscaper, he decided that his best alternative would be a lawn care business. Of course, the modification in financial status caused by his career change was the final blow to his marriage.

At the time of the incident, Pete and his wife, Joanne, a statuesque brunette, had a nine-year-old boy and a two-year-old girl together. Prior to the incident with Natalie, and before she obtained the injunction against him, he had cared for all three of the children at least three days a week while she was at work. Joanne had agreed to this for over a year *after* the incident! Yet during the divorce, after the injunction, for months she prohibited him from seeing the children *at all*. To increase his frustration, she paid babysitters to watch the children every night while she worked.

During the litigation and his separation from Joanne, Pete began dating another woman — Debi, a chunky little blonde who believed strongly in his innocence and who extremely supportive. She brought him in to see me and paid for his consultation. (In fact, during the time that I represented him, she became pregnant, because what he needed was yet another child . . . *not*).

He lived with her and her five-year old daughter in a safe neighborhood. Nevertheless, Joanne refused to allow Pete to share time with the children, even if that time was supervised by Debi and was not overnight. Furthermore, she discouraged telephone contact between him and the children. She purposely delayed the divorce process to prevent him any contact with them and to gain an upper hand in the litigation. The longer the case dragged on, the more desperate Pete became to at least *see* his children, and the more willing he was to capitulate on other issues such as how they would divide up the assets, and how much child support he would pay.

It took us months to schedule mediation. Joanne, or her attorney, kept finding reasons to delay it. Then during mediation, it seemed to us that she refused to negotiate reasonably. Her demands were completely unrelated to how a judge might resolve their issues if we actually had to go to trial.

Around this time, Pete's still-pregnant girlfriend sent him packing, and informed us that she would no longer pay his invoices. We withdrew while he still owed us money, because he could no longer afford our services, and we could not afford to work for free.

It was almost amusing when Debi called my office to schedule a consultation, seeking to retain us to file a paternity suit against Pete. Of course, we couldn't even consider such a thing; it was clearly a conflict of interest.

Pervert or drunk . . . . I still wonder.

CHAPTER EIGHT
Goals and Interests

When the collaborative team members meet with the clients for the first time, the neutral facilitator begins by asking the participants to describe their goals, what they would like to accomplish in their divorce. Then she explains and emphasizes the importance of understanding the difference between a position and a goal or an interest. An example of a position is, "I want the house," while the actual goals or interests are, "I want the kids to be near their friends; I want them in the best school system; I need a house that has room for my office in it." Another example of a position is "I want permanent alimony," while the true goal or interest is, "I want financial stability."

A position is a specific demand. An interest is the reason at the heart of the position taken. Increased stress often masks the true motives that influence people to take the positions that they do. The interest is the underlying concern or need, more general than a position, and therefore open to interpretation. Interest-based negotiation is a collaborative method which encourages the clients to understand where the other spouse is "coming from."

Position-based negotiation is an adversarial approach that considers only one side, "what I want." It limits each person to considering only his or her wants and needs, and restricts the negotiation process like blinders inhibit the eyesight of a horse.

Focusing on positions, rather than on interests, hampers settlement options. A collaborative team focuses the participants on achieving their goals, rather than on demanding their positions. By helping each person define his or her goals, the team can generate multiple settlement options to accomplish each one. Articulating goals expands the bargaining parameters and enables spouses to understand that there is more than one way to resolve their divorce issues. By prioritizing goals, the team can work towards achieving each person's most important objectives and can then agree to compromise on less important ones.

Also, couples who spend time identifying their big-picture goals at the outset will be likely to see that they share many common interests and concerns, which will play an important role in achieving the best possible outcome for both of them.

Although people undergoing a divorce are, by definition, in conflict, by focusing on interests rather than on positions, they are able to negotiate reasonably, without using threats, intimidation, or ultimatums. If one of them insists on a specific outcome, she is taking a position, rather than negotiating an interest. If the other person takes the opposite position, which they almost always do, the participants will deadlock. However, if they discuss each other's fundamental interests, they are likely to uncover different outcomes. They will identify goals and brainstorm several options to achieve them, rather than adhering to a single choice that satisfies only one position.

Consider the many layers of an onion. Positions are the outer skin and the superficial layers close to the outer skin. They are shallow and not as connected to the core because of their obvious proximity to the surface. They are simply too accessible to be useful. Like the onion, the strong and real flavor of a party's interests is found deep, many layers below the surface, closer to the heart. By actively listening to the participants, asking questions, and reframing their comments, the facilitator peels the onion, coming to the heart of the matter and their core interests, rather than their superficial positions.

At each person's first individual meeting with the team facilitator, when she asks him to describe his goals for his divorce, to assist him, she may ask him to visualize how he felt when he was first married, when he was in love and excited about the future. She will ask him to close his eyes and to remember how he felt back then. She will talk in a soothing voice, trying to relax him as much as possible. She may dim the lights and/or ask him to lie down. This serves to remind the participants of the commitments they made to one another and of the positive intentions they had back then. She may ask how they would have felt back then if a trusted friend had said, "I know this is unthinkable, but divorce does occur, and it might happen to you and your new spouse. Loving your spouse as you do today, what promises would you make about how you will behave if you should have to divorce some day?" She might ask how they would have responded.

If the party responds negatively or positionally, the facilitator may choose to take him back even farther. "What qualities in your spouse did you first fall in love with? Her sense of humor? Her good nature? What did you two have in common? What did you enjoy doing together back then? How did she make you feel? Can you recall those feelings for me here today?"

The facilitator may then ask the participant to describe his or her wedding day. "What feelings did you have? Excitement? Love? Why did you feel that way? Can you remember how that felt? Can you recall those feelings for me here today?"

Perhaps the facilitator will then request other details about the marriage in order to elicit a positive response. "How did you feel on your first anniversary? How did you feel on the day when your child was born?"

The facilitator will tread carefully with these questions, looking for but avoiding possible hot button issues.

Once the individual reaches a place where he is remembering the past fondly, the facilitator will again ask what his goals are for the divorce. The key to uncovering the party's underlying interest is to link the solution to the interest to be solved. The facilitator may need to guide the participant by offering examples of goals that are more profound than quantifiable rewards like houses and bank accounts. Such core interests may be:

1. To achieve a fair and equitable process and outcome for both of us;

2. To have enough time to think about the process and the choices before making decisions that will impact my outcome;

3. To maintain a realistic, reasoned, and positive focus during the process;

4. To parent my children during both school time and vacation time;

5. To be able to effectively co-parent with my soon-to-be-ex;

6. To maintain my financial stability, both in the present, and in the future;

7. To meet my financial responsibilities while still being incentivized to work hard;

8. To be able to choose my occupation for personal satisfaction instead of because I'm burdened with paying lifelong support;

9. To communicate better with my soon-to-be-ex-wife or husband;

10. To ensure that my divorce has as little negative impact on my children as possible;

11. To continue to be a role model for my kids;

12. To remain friendly towards and cooperative with my spouse;

13. To maintain my relationships with my in-laws; and

14. To be at peace at the end of this process.

Participants should be encouraged to think about what truly matters to them, more than anything else, regardless of whether it relates to the divorce. They can then focus on which of these broader goals or interests they want to achieve through the divorce process.

The team will encourage the participants to focus on life after divorce. "Imagine your life no longer anchored to your spouse. What does it look like three years from now? Where are you living? What are you doing for fun? Are you dating? If so, what will you look for in a date? What do you think will matter to you ten years from now?" This helps the participants to separate their immediate, short-term goals from their critical, long-term goals.

The team will propose "process anchors," questions that encourage each person to remain on the high road. These are queries like "How would I act right now if I knew that my child will watch a recording of me in this meeting ten years from now?" and "What if I had to explain my actions to my parents or my clergy?"

Sometimes one of the participants seems unable or unwilling to identify his or her goals. She simply may not know what they are, may distrust her spouse, may believe she's making herself vulnerable if she shares her interests, or she may be so focused on positions that she *cannot* identify them. The facilitator might remind her then that it is in her best interest to reach a settlement agreement that meets both participants' most important interests.

The facilitator will explain that this ensures that each party will be more willing to abide by such an agreement, and that there will then be less drama after the divorce.

In addition, settlement negotiations in which a person's highest priorities remain unaddressed waste time and money because they will refuse to sign an agreement that does not meet their most compelling concerns.

Further, when participants are aware of each other's desires, they can more effectively negotiate because they can trade interests to achieve the most satisfactory combination for both. Remind the participants that big-picture concerns, such as stability for their children and long-term financial security, really should be the most important goals.

Once goals have been defined, the collaborative professionals will remind the participating couple of these routinely, throughout the process. Each full team meeting will begin by reviewing them. Participants will each be asked to focus on the other's goals. When one person gets stuck on a position, or when the negotiations are not proceeding as effectively as they should, the team will remind the participants' of their goals and will brainstorm options to achieve those goals.

By negotiating interests rather than positions, couples are more likely to reach a mutually satisfying settlement agreement that they can and will abide by going forward.

Husband Identifying Goals

Wife Identifying Goals

This is a story a facilitator told me one day while we shared a glass of wine at a local eatery. She utilizes her skills in a number of different process venues; she engages in marriage and couples counseling, in parent coordinating for high conflict couples who are unable to communicate after litigating their disputes for so long, and in testifying about the parties' comparative abilities to parent their children when the judge needs an expert's help to determine how much time the parents should share with their children until they reach adulthood.

As time goes by, she spends more and more time as a facilitator in our CP cases. To hear her tell it, this was one of her "defining moments" in the collaborative process.

The Gift

Jillian's youngest daughter had just turned 22 years old by the time Jillian hired a divorce lawyer. I don't know if she had held off on asking for a divorce that she had wanted for some time, or if this was a recent development in her life. She had married young, for love, and was still only 53 years old. Perhaps this was her mid-life crisis.

She was attractive, with short auburn hair she wore in a loose wave down to her shoulders and a trim figure that belied the three girls she had born and raised into adulthood through their tempestuous individuations. At one point, she explained to me that she worked out every day, religiously. I don't believe that I ever saw her without at least a little blush and mascara on.

She retained counsel who explained to her the gamut of cooperative divorce options, in addition to the obvious, simply declaring war and asking a judge to decide. From these, she had selected collaborative practice to resolve the issues involved in separating the many minute details of her life from that of her husband.

I understood why collaborative divorce made sense. Her husband did not want the divorce. Collaborative practice was the only option that would address all three aspects of dissolving their marriage: the legal, of course; the financial, as did all the other choices; but also the emotional element of extricating her life from his.

She had another concern. They shared three adult daughters who were close to and would always honor him as their father. She did not want to betray them by putting private complaints about her life with him in a court file that anyone off the street could access.

Finally, there were difficulties in her case, or, as I like to say, "there was hair on it." Her husband, Tom, had always worked in the family business. Over the years, his father, the patriarch and chief executive officer of Virtuosity, Inc., had regularly gifted him, as well as his brothers, shares of the corporation's publicly traded stock. Although Thomas, Sr. had loved Jillian like a daughter, and, in fact, had absolutely doted on her, these gifts had been made specifically to "Tom," not to the married couple, "Tom and Jillian." Thomas had recently passed away, and the stocks were, without any question, "extramarital"; they were not part of the marital estate, which would be equitably distributed between the two of them in any litigated divorce.

Thus, if the assets were divided up by a court, as the law would dictate, Jillian would receive very little.

Another concern was the fact that Tom did not make a great deal of money; in the last few years, his income had been impacted by the downturn in the economy. So, regardless of her need, his ongoing contribution to Jillian's post-divorce lifestyle would be limited by his ability to pay, despite any assets he might retain.

Tom had swiftly agreed to a collaborative approach. His lawyer shared with me that Tom had been hopeful that, through the process, he would be able to convince Jillian to reconcile, which occasionally happens in a collaborative divorce.

Jillian was therefore entering into a negotiation in which she was at a disadvantage; it made sense to utilize a process that would level the playing field. Initially, I was surprised that Tom signed the collaborative participation agreement. It had taken him some time to find a lawyer to begin with. Or perhaps he was just dragging his feet. It surprised me but he agreed that, if the collaboration failed, and the participants ended up in court, his lawyer was off the case, and he would have to start from scratch, finding a new lawyer to represent him in court.

Of course, Jillian agreed to the same terms.

The two lawyers were both collaboratively-trained. I had worked with one of them many times before, but the other was brand-new to the process. She had never worked a collaborative case before, and was well-known for her prowess in the trial court. Nevertheless, when Brad suggested me as the mental health professional, the neutral facilitator to manage the process for the party and for the team, she immediately deferred to him, knowing that he had concluded several collaborative divorces successfully. They designated a CPA with whom I had worked in the past as our financial neutral and that was our core team.

As always, I met beforehand with each party separately to discuss their goals for the process and to get a feel for what was going on beneath the surface. We had debated the difference between identifying their "interests" as opposed to taking their "positions." Both of the participants seemed anxious but well-intentioned. Neither appeared to suffer from any ongoing personality disorder or mental illness that would affect their abilities to participate meaningfully.

In our one-to-one meetings, Jillian had informed me that her goal, her primary interest was to purchase a tiny condominium so that she would be able to pay all of her bills and still have money for emergencies. She would ask her girls to let *her* visit *them* rather than the reverse; she envisioned a condo that small. Given the clients' marital assets, she was aware that it did not appear that there would be enough money for her to purchase the condo outright; she would have to pay a mortgage.

Tom didn't want the divorce. But if he had no choice, and we discussed that he did not in a no-fault divorce state, then he wanted to ensure that he could stay in his home and that his children would be unaffected.

The full team (both participants, both of their lawyers, the financial neutral, and I) met a few days later in my big conference room. After reviewing and signing the collaborative participation agreement, we explored the clients' goals, as well as the process participation protocols. The protocols were no surprise to the participants; their lawyers had already given them copies for their review prior to the meeting.

That first meeting took just under the two hours we had scheduled for it, and the team professionals met afterwards for fifteen minutes to debrief.

"They are both clearly concerned that their divorce not impact their kids." I remarked, as soon as everyone was settled in my office. "I heard her loud and clear on that. Tom didn't say much, but he's already told me that's his concern, as well." I hesitated before continuing, "I think his not speaking up is because he's waiting to see where this is going to go. She's the one who wants the divorce; he's letting her take the lead oar."

"Well, you know he's hoping to reconcile," said Rina, his lawyer, the one fresh to collaborative.

"That's not happening," Brad responded. "She's been wanting to start a new life for some time, and she's already committed to it. That's her motivating interest. As you know, she's already signed a contract to purchase a one-bedroom condo downtown."

I thought it was important that his lawyer, at least, be realistic about the likelihood of reconciliation. "Rina, she's already emotionally disengaged from him. The only reason we're here, instead of in court, is because Brad explained to her how much more quickly this was likely to go than waiting to get her heard by a judge, how much less painful and damaging this process usually is, not just for the clients but also for all the interested bystanders, i.e. their kids, friends, neighbors, and extended family members, and how much less it generally costs." I added, "And I think the confidentiality element is important to her, not so much for herself as for their girls and for him."

I brought to everyone's attention some of the participants' body language I had observed. We discussed with the team how to facilitate the conversation between the clients going forward. We adjourned shortly thereafter.

We had assigned everyone homework at the end of the first meeting. Both lawyers and their clients spent considerable time marshalling the information on the clients' marital assets and liabilities. It's striking how common it is that people have no clue what they own or how much it's worth. Tracking down statements for every bank account, every credit card, every retirement account, every share of stock, and every insurance policy, to name just the most typical, can take an aggravating amount of time. Here, it was Tom who controlled the vast majority of the financial information, and he didn't want the divorce to begin with. In fact, Brad had to call Rina several times to encourage her to light a fire under him.

Once that was finally accomplished, the clients had each separately met with the financial neutral, who had put together several different possible distribution schemes for discussion at the second full team meeting. Jillian had already moved out. There was so little to argue over, we rapidly moved on to the support issue.

There it became clear that, no matter what the distribution, because Tom's income was so limited, Jillian would be living hand-to-mouth. Our discussion went round and round. Finally, we adjourned and I requested that our financial guy examine any possibility for "expanding the pie," for finding ways to maximize the income stream to both clients.

Soon it was our third full team meeting. We had worked through all of the minor issues, the personal property and items of sentimental value. We had settled the equitable distribution. Jillian would receive half of the relatively modest holdings; she would get more cash because Tom was to stay in the marital home.

Again, it was time to turn to the alimony issue. Tom simply did not make enough to support two families; it had been difficult enough to support his wife and their three girls when they were growing up. And, as everyone knows, two people who are separated cost more than a married couple, living together.

Jillian had not had a job for 30 years. The team had recommended a vocational evaluation, which she had completed. The prognosis was still not good; she would be earning little more than minimum-wage. In court, the judge will look at the need of the one party and the ability to pay of the other. Here, Jillian's need was great, but Tom's ability to pay was extremely limited. The court can't (well, shouldn't) order someone to pay more than he is capable of paying. We all knew this, including Tom. We had all discussed the various options, and had concluded that the most that Tom could pay in alimony, coupled with her own projected income, was still not enough for Jillian to afford her upkeep and a mortgage on the condo.

Everyone at the table was sweating. We had hammered out an agreement with which no one was happy. Jillian had wanted the divorce; Tom had not. Jillian would have a hard time surviving on what Tom had offered, but it was all she could expect. We took a break.

When we came back to the conference room, Jillian was resigned. No one was happy and no one could look anyone else in the eye. Tom entered last, following on his lawyer's heels. As she settled in her seat, he stood behind his own chair and clenched the back of it tightly. Although he was older than Jillian, he stood straight-backed, grey-haired but without the belly that usually accompanied middle age.

"I have an offer to make to Jillian."

His lawyer sat up, plainly taken aback by this surprise announcement. He continued, "I own a number of shares of stock in my father's business that we have all agreed are non-marital. However, there is no question in my mind that my father meant those shares to benefit both of us, and that, had he known what would've happened, he would have gifted them to both of us. I want to honor his intention and give half of my shares in Virtuosity to Jillian."

To this day, I still do not know what drove Tom's decision. Perhaps he hoped to win her back. Perhaps he had finally realized the marriage was over. Perhaps he wanted his kids to believe that he would always "do the right thing." I can only say that the team that day was so taken aback that no one was able to immediately respond.

Finally Jillian said, "Tom, I can't express my appreciation for your generosity. I hope you'll never regret it. I will always respect you for it. You did the best you could in our marriage, and I hope you understand that I know that. We have three beautiful kids because of it. Thank you."

Our clients do the strangest things to each other while they struggle in the grip of the emotional tempest created by divorce. When they default to the traditional option, there is no professional involved in the process to help address this intense stress, and the sometimes consequent inability to make decisions rationally.

We trial lawyers aren't always able to watch the story play out to the end. Sometimes the client finds it impossible to follow his lawyer's instructions. In other cases, he cannot continue to fund the legal fees incurred in divorce court. Happily, we were able to stick this one out to its finish. But we never did figure out what possessed our client's wife to do what she did. Here's how he tells the story.

The Mercedes

As you watch the woman you love delicately making her way down the aisle to you, you never expect she will become your worst nightmare. Ten years into my marriage with Mariela, the woman for whom I had once baked cookies (in a lame attempt at romance), now gave me cold sweats. We agreed to divorce; it was the last time we truly agreed on anything, and it was not pretty. Unfortunately, when you get caught up in an emotional tornado, you'll agree to anything just to escape. Two years later, when the dust had finally settled, I realized that the final divorce agreement had to be modified. I had let myself be taken advantage of, simply to avoid getting sucked up in the maelstrom.

In our divorce agreement, Mariela had been given primary residential responsibility of our twelve-year-old, Robert. However, he had lived mostly with me since then. She must have discovered a new lease on life – she was going out a lot and a kid probably put a damper on this. I was happy with this arrangement – he and I were close. However, during those two years, I continued to pay child support and never informed the court of the changed circumstances. She would insist he move back in with her if I attempted to modify anything. As long as I continued to pay child support, she happily let Robert live with me. But now, I was done!

But wait! There's more! In our divorce, I had been ordered to pay Mariela's mortgage by direct payment to the mortgagee. (This would never have happened without us agreeing to it first, but I had wanted to ensure that the mortgage got paid; my name was on it.) As the real estate taxes and insurance were rolled into the payment, I paid those as well, though not ordered to do so.

My divorce lawyer had failed to appreciate this conundrum at the time. To be fair, in my frantic attempt to escape, I did as well. To remedy this, my new lawyer requested that my alimony be reduced by the amount of the taxes and insurance – a reasonable request, *I* thought. I also sought custody of Robert and to modify child support accordingly. Mariela, of course, hired an expensive Rambo lawyer to fight me, despite that she had been fine with me having actual custody for the past two years.

It took a year to get a final hearing on the judge's calendar. In the meantime, her counsel racked up fees with unnecessary formalities. This translated to costs for me because my own lawyer had to rack up time responding. Not to mention all *my* time off of work for meetings with him. For example, Mariela's attorney scheduled my deposition. I didn't bother having her deposed – we knew everything there was to know about each other. But he scheduled me for three whole hours. Not only was that three hours for both attorneys, but my lawyer had to prep me for it, too.

On the day of my depo, I showed up at the appointed time and place, sat down, and readied myself for the dirty laundry to be aired. After a few formalities, he got right to it. "What's Robert's favorite color?" he asked, tapping his pencil on his legal pad.

I hesitated, raising my eyebrows. *Robert's favorite color?* I thought to myself. *What does that have to do with anything?*

I recalled my attorney's advice to meet the opposing lawyer eye-to-eye and to answer his questions directly. "Blue," I stated.

"What is Robert's favorite food?" he asked right away, jotting down my answer to the last question.

"Macaroni and Cheese." I was starting to wonder where this was headed.

"What's Robert's favorite game?"

I hesitated again, thinking that these were silly questions and a waste of my time. But I remembered my attorney advising me not to rush, to be polite, and to understand what was being asked of me. I realized these questions were ways of seeing how well I knew Robert. I also remembered my attorney's advice not to guess

— that "I don't know" is a perfectly acceptable answer, if it is true.

"I don't know," I answered. "Two weeks ago it was soccer, but this week he's been more interested in basketball. It changes."

The deposition droned on and on. It was a relief when it was over. Thank god, my attorney felt no need to ask me anything.

I only wished that was the end of the dispute.

After the divorce, I was also required to pay Mariela's lease payments on a C240 Mercedes-Benz. I could deduct those payments from the alimony I paid, so long as she possessed the C240 and there were recurring lease payments. I later purchased a new car, and we agreed she would give me the C240 and take my previous car, a SL 500 Mercedes-Benz, which was a better vehicle.

A week after Mariela took possession of my beloved SL 500, I received a phone call from her while I was at work. "Allen, you have a problem!"

"Mariela, I'm at work and I just had to leave a meeting. I don't have time for games." I was exasperated. "What do you mean, I have a problem?"

"We-e-ell," she drew it out, "I was in an accident."

"What?!" I exclaimed. "Are you okay? What happened? Was anybody hurt?" And yes, this barrage of questions concerning the well-being of my ex-wife rushed out of me before my thoughts *even turned* to the condition of the car.

"Yes, yes. I'm fine. I got into a tiny spat with one of the drivers because they're all saying it was my fault. But, whatever," she calmly told me. "That's not your problem. It's your car."

"My car? What?" I continued on, dumbfounded.

"It was pretty banged up after the accident."

"Oh," I said, starting to gather my wits, "that's fine. The insurance will help. I'm just glad nobody was hurt." Ever the caring guy, I know! But I'd be lying if I said I wasn't a little dismayed at the thought of the car being damaged – a cracked headlight, her shiny silver paint marred with scratches. I was a "wax and clay bar every month" kind of guy.

"No, Allen. The car *was* banged up a bit in the accident," she told me. "But *then* – well . . . I moved it."

"It '*was*' banged up a bit, but '*then*'?" I repeated, questioningly.

A brief laugh. "I must have left it on a railroad track...."

She let that hang. I had a feeling that she was enjoying this on some level. I quietly waited for her to explain, as the image of me patiently buffing out a few scratches over the weekend quickly dissolved from my mind. "It got hit by a train, Allen. It's wrecked."

I didn't say much after that.

Turns out Mariela had agreed to obtain insurance for the SL 500 in our lease agreement, but she had never done so, and thus her insurance company denied her claim. *My* insurance company only reimbursed me $17,000 of the $31,000 in repairs.

After the accident, I returned the C240 to her (she needed a car), while I still paid the lease, $600/month. My insurer dropped me, and my new coverage cost me $8,000 more per year. And I was still paying the lease on the wrecked SL 500 of $1,700/month.

In the end, I ended up with custody. The judge ordered Mariela to pay support, which I didn't want. However, my attorney explained that child support belongs to the child, not the parent.

I had faced the tornado head on; it cost me thousands of dollars *and* my beloved Mercedes. However, afterwards, as Robert and I played basketball, I realized the peace of mind was worth it.

Judges Are Not Therapists

Judges like to pontificate, "In criminal court, we see bad people at their best; in family court, we see good people at their worst." I am grateful to the lawyer who shared this story; so many of us have been privileged to participate in a collaborative divorce that revealed good people at their best.

The Agreement

I had a client, John, who had been married for twenty-eight years. He was a portly but tidy man. We met for the first time in July. It was at least 93 degrees outside, but, no matter the weather (as I discovered over time), he always wore a crisp, long-sleeved, button-down, collared shirt with a pair of beige slacks and tasseled dress shoes. His clothing was always neatly pressed, and his thinning hair in place. Despite his weight, he never seemed to sweat or appear ruddy. When we shook hands, his palm was dry and cool. Even though we were discussing a divorce that he clearly did not want, he was quick to smile and laugh. I immediately liked him. Within five minutes of our first meeting, my dog was on his lap, enjoying his attention. If Hachi approved, I approved.

I explained to him that, unfortunately, it only takes one person to get a divorce. Once I'd clarified that unhappy fact, he realized his options were limited. He brought me the letter he'd received from Peggy, his wife's attorney. In it, she had suggested a collaborative approach to the dissolution of their marriage, and offered him the names of several practitioners. I was the third he interviewed. While his anger about the divorce seemed unconstrained, even infinite at times, he agreed to handle the divorce collaboratively and ultimately retained me.

He earned significantly more than his wife, Sara. His elderly parents lived in a separate apartment at the family residence, as did their adult disabled son, John's younger brother, Jim. After they each met with her, Mary, a facilitator with whom I'd worked before, shared their goals with the rest of the collaborative team members. According to Mary, John's goals in the divorce were to retain the home so that his family could continue to reside in it with him, to have enough extra income to cover the care they required, and to maintain as good a relationship with Sara as possible.

Her goals were to have financial security and to leave the marriage with John still as a good friend.

Both John and Sara shared an interest in protecting his parents and his brother, and hoped that John could afford to keep the house. If not, his parents would end up in an assisted living facility — not a happy prospect — and they would need to find somewhere else for Jim to reside, as well.

The first meeting was a teleconference. Professionals act so much more politely during the collaborative process than they do in litigation. Although somewhat unorthodox in the collaborative model, Mary asked the attorneys to explain what they felt their clients would receive if they litigated. Peggy believed that if we litigated the case, Sara might receive as much as $4,000/month indefinitely in spousal support. I was convinced that the figure was closer to $3,500/month, but otherwise agreed with Peggy.

The first full team meeting was held at Mary's office in a space fitted out like a living room, filled with comfortable overstuffed chairs, which had been dragged into a circle to face each other. Mary offered the professionals small side tables for our computers, but for the most part, there was large open space surrounded by the chairs. The facilitator explained that the vulnerable set-up helped the participants to understand that they were to be open and transparent. Acting the host, Mary guided us to our chairs so that John and Sara sat beside their respective attorneys. They sat across from one another, the lawyers faced each other, and the two neutrals (Mary and our financial professional, Matt) sat across from one another.

We discussed the participation agreement before we signed it. Then Mary asked the clients to describe their goals, as identified when they had each met with her, to the team. We discussed the collaborative process further. Because they hadn't had an opportunity to meet with Matt or to exchange financial "discovery" (the legal term for the information to be shared), we wrapped up a bit early with homework to be accomplished before our second meeting. Both were instructed to consult with our neutral financial professional and then to provide him with any documents he didn't already have.

After they did this, but prior to the second meeting, the professionals met again to discuss the status. I was apprehensive that Sara expected too much alimony to meet their joint goal of allowing John to keep the house. However, Matt relieved my fears by detailing his recent conversation with her. (Peggy had accompanied her because Sara was uncertain of what to expect and had invited her.)

Matt explained that Sara was very concerned with maintaining her standard of living. "I just don't want to feel like I'm taking a step back in life, you know what I mean?" Sara said.

"When you split one household into two, each party will inevitably have a reduction in income," he had reasoned.

Peggy said, "And wasn't one of your interests that John be able to keep the home so that his parents and brother wouldn't be uprooted? Do you think that he can afford to keep the home and pay you enough to maintain your standard of living?"

"Well, no," Sara admitted.

"Can you envision yourself living in a smaller, less expensive home?" Matt asked.

"Yes, I suppose that would be nice. I do hate cleaning up that big home and after all of those people. It will be easier to only have myself to take care of, and I guess I don't need all of that room."

"You mentioned your goal of financial security," Matt reminded her. "Could you reduce your standard of living, and the amount of money that you need from John, and achieve that?

She thought for a moment. Matt and Peggy could almost see the wheels spinning. "If I have a smaller home, I don't really need all that money from John. If I'm not caring for his family, I could increase my hours at work. In a few years, I'll get social security, too."

She quickly came to grips with the fact that, by the time her husband bought out her interest in the family residence, and paid alimony of $3,500/month or more, he wouldn't be able to afford to keep the house. And maybe she didn't need him to.

Sara knew that if she insisted on "her due," he'd be unable to remain in the home. By the end of the second meeting, they had decided that Sara would receive $2,500/month for the first year and that it would decrease by $500/month each subsequent year, until it went to $0 in year six. They agreed that the court would retain jurisdiction over the issue of support in the event that Sara's circumstances changed. (This would also have been true if they had litigated the case and she had received $3,500 or more.)

They also agreed that they would each receive 50% of the marital assets. They were uncertain of their home's value, so they agreed to have it appraised. The financial neutral recommended a reputable appraiser who specialized in valuing homes in the area, and they decided to use him and to pay the fee from marital funds. With limited liquid assets, they determined that John would buy-out Sara's interest in the family residence by refinancing the property, liquidating some of the equity they had built up during their marriage.

Each would pay their respective attorney's fees and share 50/50 the fees of the other neutral professionals. Because we had handled the divorce collaboratively, each one only owed around $10,000. (Had we gone to court, their fees would have easily reached $100,000 each.)

At the end of our second full team meeting, we'd worked out everything, and established that I would prepare the first draft of the paperwork evidencing their agreement to be signed at the final meeting, as well as the final judgment approving it.

The following day, guess which party tried to renege on the deal that had not even been inked yet?

John.

I asked him "why?" He just looked at the floor and shrugged.

I tried to explain to him that in litigation Sara would still receive 50% of the marital property, as well as probably $3,500/month in alimony, that he would most likely have to pay a share of her attorney's fees and costs, *and* that both of them would incur significantly greater expense. In other words, I clarified that he stood to gain nothing by breaking the deal and that he would almost certainly end up worse off.

He still wanted to call off the deal. I put my analysis in writing and emailed it to him, but to no avail.

I racked my brains to figure out why he would back out of an agreement which clearly favored him. I called Mary and discussed any number of possibilities:

1. Sara had committed indiscretions during the marriage, and he may not have wanted to let her off the hook so easily. She had several emotional affairs during their relationship. She blamed him for working too much and not being there for her. He never truly forgave her. Each time he came close to forgiving her, she would admit to another emotional affair. While these were irrelevant in a traditional courtroom divorce, absent her spending marital funds on someone outside the marriage, this might have been an interest infringing on his ability to accept the agreement we had fashioned.

2. John was a proud guy. Perhaps he was ashamed to accept what he believed to be her charity in the terms of the agreement. He had always taken care of her financially, and it was hard for him to come to grips with the fact that he couldn't continue to do so at the same level going forward.

3. He did not want a divorce. Maybe he was just not ready for the marriage to be over, and, by refusing to agree to the settlement, he could slow down the process. Because he blamed her for the divorce, perhaps he wanted to withhold what she wanted, i.e. an end to the marriage.

4. During the marriage, she shouldered much of the caregiving responsibility for his parents and brother. John never wanted to fulfill that role. He was comfortable working hard and paying the bills, while Sara cared for his family. Once divorced, he would have to take a more active role in their care, and maybe he didn't want or wasn't ready for that.

Fortunately, this divorce wasn't in mediation, but in collaboration. I sent John back to the facilitator. She was able to get the deal back on track because his issues were emotional and she was trained to deal with human behavior and interpersonal dynamics.

Soon after, John signed the marital settlement agreement.

Later I asked her how she had dealt with whatever had been going on in my client's head. She had brought him back into her office and reviewed his goals. They had included having the financial means to keep the home so that his family was not uprooted, protecting his parents and brother, and maintaining a good relationship with Sara. She counseled him to "focus on the outcome you designed." She asked him to tell her the story of how he envisioned his future without his wife and thereby helped him frame that picture in terms of his goals. She advised him not to be sidetracked by outside issues. "Stay in your lane and you can get there," she told him.

During the process John had made discoveries about himself that made him uncomfortable. That discomfort infected the settlement agreement in his vision. Truth be told, he really didn't want caregiver responsibility for his parents and brother. He loved them and wanted to keep them close, but couldn't fathom his life when he took on all of those duties. He had a hard time admitting this even to himself because he felt it was a betrayal of the family he loved. However, once he'd separated the cause of his discomfort from his agreement with Sara, and accepted it, he was able to sign.

Had this case been handled in any other process not involving a facilitator or coach, a mental health professional, the settlement would have fallen apart. John and Sara's underlying needs, interests, values, and goals would not have been satisfied. Unfortunately, perfectly reasonable and even beneficial settlement options are rejected all the time only because people's stress and their emotions get in the way and they aren't able to think clearly. But in the collaborative process, we can make it happen because those emotions *are* addressed.

CHAPTER NINE
Brainstorming

Brainstorming settlement ideas is a crucial component of the collaborative process. CP provides an open environment that encourages everyone on the team to participate. The participants should feel as though their thoughts are being heard and their interests validated.

Collaborative professionals will encourage active listening in a casual environment. If team members are relaxed enough to chat and crack jokes, then they'll produce more creative ideas. On the other hand, too much levity raises concerns for the divorcing couple that their concerns aren't being taken seriously, so collaborative professionals will be conscious of the fine line between comfortable enough to encourage creativity, and not so relaxed as to disconcert the clients.

The brainstorming step follows the clients' identification of goals and interests. The objective is to answer the question, "how do we satisfy these interests and resolve inevitable conflicts between the two people?" Brainstorming should be a fast-paced exercise in which the participants do not have time to self-evaluate or to form preconceptions about options. Ideas should be tossed out to the group in an uninhibited, creative fashion.

Someone on the collaborative team will pull out the chalkboard or the flipchart and the multicolored pens. One team member will be appointed to record every idea, taking brief notes so that ideas are not forgotten or misplaced, and team members are able to build on ideas that have already been mentioned and noted on the board.

No suggestion is a "bad" one; there are no bad ideas in brainstorming. The team should be encouraged to think "outside the box" and discouraged from criticizing any of the ideas, especially at this time. Evaluation of ideas is a different process from the creative brainstorming process. Encourage the participants to suggest even "ridiculous" ideas, because these may well lead to more fruitful options.

Avoid evaluation at this point to sustain receptivity to all the potential alternatives. Judgment and analysis stunt idea generation and limit creativity. Offering a wide variety of options that later can be compared and contrasted to each other, which in turn sometimes leads to options yet unidentified, ultimately leads to the best chance of reaching a settlement that addresses the clients' most important concerns and interests.

Before brainstorming, the professionals are likely to remind participants of their goals, encourage them to forget about their positions, and coach them to focus on their interests. They will urge the divorcing couple to explore options, even if they do not feel that they are feasible alternatives (no self-evaluation here either!). Sometimes ideas that seem completely unlikely lead to very reasonable (and accepted) solutions. However, while it is good to keep an open mind, it is also important to separate participants from positions that are absolutely unacceptable.

When later evaluating option ideas, the collaborative professionals will discuss with the clients the ideas of BATNA (the best alternative to a negotiated agreement) and WATNA (the worst alternative to a negotiated agreement). A party should not expect that he or she will receive his or her best alternative or that the other participant will agree to his or her worst alternative. They should recognize their settlement ranges; at this stage, the professionals will work hard to deflate either side's inflated expectations.

In brainstorming, small components are easier to manage than large issues, so implement a course of baby steps. Begin brainstorming by discussing what choices are already working for the spouses. Next, develop objective standards for a plausible agreement. Talk openly and frankly, bouncing ideas off of one another. Discuss reasonable hypothetical scenarios. Here the professionals will suggest alternative approaches that have worked in other cases, bringing their expertise to the table.

Consider that left-brained thinkers and right-brained thinkers brainstorm differently, and the team is likely to have both participating. While left-brained thinkers benefit less from a cluttered process, right-brained thinkers don't shy away from chaos. Be aware that the note taker is likely to record based on which "brain" he utilizes most. His approach may stress some of the folks in the room, so, while he should be efficient, he should also try to do so in a way that appeals to both types of individuals.

The team should limit itself to a specific period of time or number of ideas for this session. This will maintain the quick pace of brainstorming, which is important when generating options.

Once the participants have given many ideas, begin to tweak and trade possibilities in order to move toward the final settlement. Evaluation begins here; this is the time to explore solutions further, using conventional approaches. Determine how the participants' interests can be met by the proposed solutions. Discuss the cost and benefit to each client for each item. Take time to have each step into the other's shoes and analyze whether he or she would be happy with the proposal if he or she was on the other side.

Through brainstorming, collaborative team participants are able to explore many different scenarios in their pursuit to reach an effective settlement agreement.

The Full Team Brainstorms

It's Your Choice
(Litigation versus Collaboration)

Component	Collaborative	Courtroom
Decision-maker Judge's Role	You & your spouse both control the process & make decisions; judge enters a judgment approving your agreement	A judge who doesn't know you or share your values controls the process & makes the decisions; enters a judgment that controls your life until your last child is no longer dependent
Atmosphere	Interest-based; team/goal oriented; Safe	Positional; adversarial; hostile
Degree of Adversity	You both pledge & team supports & enables mutual respect & transparency	Hostile, adversarial & disrespectful; discovery process discourages candor & transparency
Costs	Manageable expenses, usually less than litigation; team use of experts is financially efficient	Unpredictable costs often escalate rapidly; post-judgment litigation is common & costly; adversarial expert battles are financially inefficient
Timetable	You both craft the timetable, along with your collaborative team	Judge mandates timetable; crowded dockets cause delays regularly

Experts' Role	Jointly retain experts to inform & guide in developing transparent data into mutually beneficial solutions	Separate experts support your positions (@2x the expense); non-transparency requires experts to work harder
Lawyers' Role	Lawyers problem-solve to help you both generate an interests-based, "win-win" agreement	Lawyers fight to win, but someone always loses, often both, in a court-imposed, "lose-lose" judgment
Confidentiality	CP is confidential & private	Public & subject to media attention
Communication	Team educates & assists both clients to effectively communicate	Court process discourages communication between "parties"
Process Nature	Voluntary; transparent	Mandatory, *if* you do not choose another process to reach agreement; secretive & deceptive
Conflict of Interest	Lawyers are disqualified if process fails, if either of you opts for court; their *only* interest is to help you reach agreement	Lawyers profit (i.e. make more $) if you do *not* agree & continue to litigate
Skills Component	Problem-solving & communication skills	None

Winners and Losers

Negotiating Agreement Without Losing

CHAPTER TEN
Combat the Impact of Grief and Stress on Decision-Making

Divorce is one of the most stressful and emotional experiences that a person will ever endure. Not only does one process the grief over the loss of one's loved one, one's relationship, and the future that one thought one had, but one is forced to decide critical issues that will affect one's family forever in the midst of one's anguish.

Psychologists advise people to refrain from important decision-making when experiencing periods of high grief and stress, yet the divorce process forces people to make life-changing choices as quickly as possible. The longer one waits, the more one's attorney's fees mount, and the more impatient the judge becomes because one's divorce remains pending on his docket.

It is well known that a person grieving the end of a marriage experiences Kübler-Ross' five stages of grief. First, he suffers from denial; he is unable to admit that the relationship is really over. Next, he is angry at his spouse, who is leaving him, for causing him such pain. After anger, he may plead with his former companion, promising that whatever caused the breakup will never happen again. In the following phase, he may feel discouraged that his bargaining plea did not convince his former partner to stay, which may send him into depression. Finally, the grieving spouse accepts the situation, realizes that the relationship is over, and lastly is able to move on with his life. At this point, he is finally in an emotional condition to make important decisions.

Unfortunately, most people don't enjoy the luxury of being able to wait until they reach the acceptance stage to deal with their divorce.

Stress alters the way that people weigh risk and reward. Stressed individuals tend to focus more on the benefits of the alternatives that they are considering and to pay less attention to the disadvantages.

Additionally, men and women tend to handle stress differently. Where men become even more willing to take risks, women become more conservative.

Stress can have a detrimental effect on divorcing spouses.

Litigation only intensifies anxiety, and hinders the decision-making process.

When faced with the stress of divorce, it is crucial to remain as calm as possible, especially while negotiating, mediating, or testifying at depositions or hearings that are intimidating by themselves, without adding that additionally distressing element of your active participation! You should aggressively work to calm yourself by engaging in certain physical steps that will actually help to calm your emotions.

Begin by taking slow, deep breaths. Actively calming oneself is a learned skill and will improve with practice. So practice the technique at home prior to your significant divorce-related appointments. Hold your hand over your stomach. Push your hand away from your stomach as you inhale through your nose, and then allow your hand to drop back toward your stomach as you exhale through your mouth. When you are able to perform this technique well, you will not need to hold your hand over your belly. Inhale slowly, and then exhale slowly, moving your stomach rather than your shoulders and chest.

Deep breathing alone may not be sufficient to compose you, especially during highly emotional periods. If you are experiencing stress even while engaged in the abdominal breathing described above, you may need to slow down and focus on your breathing even more. Count your slow, deep breaths until you reach ten. Focus on each segment of your breathing. Be aware as you begin each inhale, and continue to remain actively focused as you reach the middle and end of the inhale. Then notice the beginning, the middle, and end of the exhale.

Being so aware of each phase of the breath helps you to remain focused on what is going on in the moment (your breathing) and distracts you from outside stressors. It prevents you from worrying about the future, thinking negative thoughts about your spouse, or rehashing destructive events from your past. Your body should begin to relax once you are completely concentrated on the present moment.

We all know that re-living hurtful events can trigger the negative emotions that we felt when those events first occurred all over again, sometimes with the same impact. Sometimes we masochistically relish going over past happenings in our minds for no good reason or purpose, like searching out a canker sore in the mouth with your tongue instead of ignoring it.

In divorce, it is important to push thoughts of upsetting events out of your mind. Change the subject. Purposely deliberate on calming thoughts to relax you during a stressful situation. List your calming thoughts ahead of time. Remind yourself that you are safe and that you control your own inner state. Tell yourself that your attorney is looking out for your best interests and won't permit you to enter into a bad deal or to look bad in court.

Calming Thoughts

- My attorney is here to protect me, to represent my interests, and to ensure that I negotiate an agreement that I can live with.
- I don't have to agree to anything that I can't live with or don't want.
- The divorce cannot be final until I am satisfied with the agreement.
- Even when my spouse is distressed or upset, I don't have to be. I am in control of my own thoughts and my own attitude.
- I can focus on calming myself even if my spouse's behavior is inappropriate.
- I need not respond immediately to anything that is said. In fact, it is best if . . .
- I will remain calm and consider my response before I speak. I will think before I speak, and I will choose my words carefully.

What positive thoughts do *you* have? What is your life like outside the divorce process? Are your kids doing well in school? Do you have great friends who support you? Do you have a wonderful job at which you excel? What do you envision your future five years *after* divorce to look like?

Even if your spouse is upset about an issue, remind yourself that you do not need to be distraught as well. Just because she is

153

acting inappropriately, remember that you do not have to mirror her poor behavior. Focus on your breathing to stay calm.

When negotiating, remember that you don't have to agree to anything with which you are not comfortable, that you are not required to respond immediately to offers or to anything said, and that your settlement cannot be finalized until you are content with the result. Repeatedly remind yourself how important it is to remain calm. Always consider your responses before you speak.

There is a less stressful alternative to litigation. CP allows individuals to set the pace for their divorce. Coaches or mental health facilitators are integral to the core collaborative team, and they understand better than other professionals when it is wise for clients to move forward, or when more time is needed for some clients to work through their grief. In litigation, if a case languishes because a party is not ready to move forward, opposing counsel may force it forward by filing upsetting and costly motions, or the judge may compel the parties to move the case along. In CP, if it is determined that a client needs more time, rather than purposely exacerbating the emotional person's stress, the team discusses this issue with the other person, and coaches her on how to alleviate her spouse's anxiety or feelings of stressful overload.

That doesn't mean that a party has unlimited time to work out their stress before proceeding, but the collaborative process helps people work through stress so that they can more quickly be in a position to negotiate meaningfully and effectively. And the other party, who may have moved forward more quickly in the grieving process, is educated as to how to act to help the grieving party move forward as quickly as possible.

A collaborative divorce will run smoothly and productively if each client is able to recognize the other's needs and wishes, and if they are each willing to look for solutions which help both of them.

Although the collaborative process may ultimately be successful, it will be unnecessarily difficult if a party insists on interrupting, on raising his or her voice throughout a meeting, or on leaving the room while others are speaking. Other difficulties that may hinder the process include a party's inability to process accurately what his or her spouse has said or to express his or her own thoughts and feelings clearly.

Collaborative practice will not work in all divorces. There is a significant risk of failure if a party is unwilling to sit in same room with his spouse for entire meetings, or is unwilling or unable to talk with his spouse or to listen to what she has to say in the safety of the team meeting. Further, the process is likely to be unsuccessful if the participants are unwilling or unable to avoid violence at all times, if one party is intimidated by the other, or if a party is lying or hiding data.

However, in most divorces, collaborative practice is a refreshing alternative to traditional litigation. The team focuses on what is best to help each party proceed, rather than attacking the enemy while he is down. Where litigation takes advantage of the vulnerable party's emotional state, collaboration is a more even-handed, relaxing method that focuses on the needs of both clients. And when clients negotiate while in a more positive state, they tend to enter into agreements that are fairer to both of them, and easier for both to perform and fulfill. This, of course, decreases the likelihood of post-judgment conflict because each spouse is happier with the end result.

Choosing to collaborate on your divorce instead of litigating against your spouse will give you a greater likelihood of remaining calm (and healthy) during your divorce process and beyond.

Collaborative Skills and Attitudes

Both collaborative participants should be:

- ✓ Prepared and able to shun violence;
- ✓ Willing to forego interrupting the other participants in order to listen;
- ✓ Able to forgive interruptions by the other participants, if they do occur;
- ✓ Able to express themselves in normal tones throughout a meeting;
- ✓ Able to forgive a participant who expresses him or herself more loudly than is necessary during a meeting;
- ✓ Capable of remaining present in the meeting

155

regardless of what is said, or of how it is communicated;

✓ Willing to confer with the other participant in the same room;

✓ Willing to forgo intimidation;

✓ Able to ignore intimidation, if it does occur;

✓ Able to openly discuss matters with the other participant and the professional team members;

✓ Capable of being transparent and open regarding matters material to the divorce; and

✓ Able to express his or her own thoughts and feelings clearly.

The collaborative divorce will be smoother and more productive if both participants work to be:

✓ Able to identify each partner's needs and wishes;

✓ Willing to brainstorm for solutions that work for both of them;

✓ Willing to "think outside the box";

✓ Capable of actively hearing and appreciating the other spouse's viewpoint;

✓ Willing to consider options other than those he or she has already volunteered or considered;

✓ Prepared to listen actively and to understand accurately what the other participant has said;

✓ Able to actively hear constructive criticism; and

✓ Able to work on modifying his or her behavior based thereon.

I am a lawyer who shares my story with my client, to establish common ground and to make it easier for him to share with me. This is one of the stories I tell.

Misnomer

I suffer from juvenile diabetes, but I didn't "come down with it" when I was a child. In December of 1989, my husband sold our home, without telling me, although ultimately I signed off on the sale. In addition, a lawyer I respected filed a pleading in federal court accusing me of professional misfeasance, because I had interviewed a "management employee" without giving the lawyer notice and an opportunity to be present at the interview.

The so-called "management employee" in question had been the deli manager at the local grocery store. He wasn't the corporate executive to whom the rule actually referred, but rather the kid who punches a time clock and works behind the counter. The only thing he "managed" was the lunch meats he wrangled into sandwiches. But the misfeasance allegation was a strategic ploy intended to throw me off balance, and it did. Seriously.

At the same time, I'd been practicing law for nine years and married for two when I came down with what I thought was a bladder infection. I raced to my doctor to get medicine for my symptoms. Little did I know.

I had been in to see him just two weeks earlier, and everything had been status quo. This time, he ran a simple blood test. After the nurse reported back to him, he sat me down in his office.

"Your blood sugar is over 400."

"So what does that mean?"

"It could mean that you've developed diabetes. I'm not sure because you don't fit the description. You're thirty-two, healthy, and a slender 118 pounds." He grimaced. "It's a mystery."

It's never good when your doctor says "it's a mystery." At the very least, it will cost you a lot of money.

My blood sugar did not come down. After several days he instructed me to go to Boston, to the Jocelyn Diabetes Center, the only one in the country back then. It was a treatment center, like a hospital, but with a week-long schedule of classes for newly diagnosed diabetics to teach them how to care for themselves. "Do not pass 'Go'; do not collect $200; just get yourself to Jocelyn *now*."

I explained why I was too busy to go. Without even considering the suit in which I had been accused of unprofessionalism, I had several major lawsuits in which I was "first chair," the primary lawyer. With my demanding schedule, I arrived at the office by 7:00 a.m. and never left before 9:00 p.m. I had quit smoking two years earlier, so I never needed a smoke break, and I rarely ate lunch away from my desk. I had no life outside of work, but I loved what I was doing. And I felt fine, except for the "bladder infection."

He argued with me, certain I'd developed juvenile diabetes, although no one in my family had it, and I was not at risk. Rather than explain, cajole, or plead, he simply insisted I go to Boston.

He probably did explain, but I couldn't hear him; my ears were congested by stress. What stress? I'd recently had the flu. Now, two weeks before Christmas, I told my husband of two years that I thought a separation would be appropriate. What I really meant was "I want a divorce," but I was afraid to tell him. Thankfully, he had sold our home out from under me, so it was *apropos* that I suggest a "separation." One step at a time, right?

And there was the "professional misfeasance" allegation. While my opposing counsel ultimately abandoned his ridiculous claim, at thirty-two I hadn't suffered the slings and arrows of personal attack that have now become so commonplace among trial attorneys.

When the doctor asked about the history of diabetes in my family, I told him there was none. Then he asked me about stress. I laughed.

It turns out that stress can cause juvenile diabetes. Who knew? And if it can cause so major a life-long illness, what can it do to the decision-making that dissolving your marital relationship requires? Collaborative divorce can help you deal with that; traditional courtroom divorce cannot.

CHAPTER ELEVEN
The Paradigm Shift

Divorce doesn't belong in the courtroom! Nor does the restructuring of families! How can it be that one buys a license to get married but one must *sue* one's spouse to obtain a divorce?

Because the collaborative process requires attorneys to focus on the interests and goals of their clients rather than on their positions, they must make a paradigm shift from how they would typically think and act as adversarial trial lawyers. Their clients pledge to be transparent, so their counsel are not allowed to participate in the "hide the discovery" games in which the trial attorneys often engage. With a single specialist retained for any particular issue, "the battle of the experts" no longer has an intrinsic or expensive role. The clients actually speak *to* each other during the meetings, making it difficult, if not impossible, for any one lawyer to "stir the pot."

Rather than breaking down the other person, the goal becomes working as a team to satisfy the most important interests of each side.

This shift challenges a seasoned litigator who steps into the role of a collaborative team member. Litigated family law cases are treated like other civil cases, without considering that the two people will need to maintain a working relationship with each other after the divorce. The adversarial court system hinders the goodwill and cooperation necessary in co-parenting relationships.

Collaborative practice replaces the evidence and procedural rules with protocols. The two individuals have much say over the process because it is viewed as *their* process. The attorney must be comfortable with relinquishing that control to the client. The lawyer helps her client identify and articulate her interests, brainstorm options to meet those interests, evaluate those options, and focus on the probable risks and rewards.

Collaborative team members usually belong to community practice groups that meet regularly to educate and confer, and these individuals often work together. They are friends, which makes it easier for the team to negotiate a positive resolution. They meet before and after full team conferences (which include professionals and clients) to discuss the best way to move the clients and the process forward. They focus their energy on being positive and efficient, rather than on being defeating and damaging.

Because these lawyers are required to withdraw if their clients choose to litigate, collaborative lawyers concentrate on successfully resolving the case. Working together, they encourage the rest of the team, including the spouses, to remain open-minded and creative.

During team meetings, an attorney may speak directly with the person who is not her client. Rather than acting oppositionally, she will try to put the other side at ease by hearing his viewpoints and empathizing with his perspectives.

While the lawyer and team may discuss the law and what could happen if one of the participants gives up and goes to court, that is just one factor that the clients must evaluate when negotiating. The attorneys try to direct them about the best choices for their families, regardless of what the law might say, assuming that the lawyer can even pinpoint what that is. While a judge will focus on the relationships between the parties and their children via a snapshot he sees at an evidentiary hearing, the parties themselves are able to take other interests into account, not just those of their children, but also those of their extended families, their friends, and other people involved in their lives. And they can evaluate those interests across a broad spectrum of their own values, with which they are intimately familiar.

Although adjusting to this paradigm shift may be uncomfortable at first, collaborative practice offers a far more rewarding and positive process, not just for the "parties" in the divorce process, but also for the professional participants.

Pauline Tesler, a pioneer of the collaborative divorce movement, told me the following story about one of her early collaborative cases. This divorce took place before she realized that collaborative clients would be better served by an interdisciplinary team than by just two lawyers, one for either client. Therefore, there were no mental health professionals nor was there a neutral financial professional on this team. It was in the late 1990s. Pauline represented the wife and worked with an attorney with whom she had already successfully concluded a few collaborative cases. I don't know the actual names of the clients or the specific details of this tale, but its essence remains.

The Ceremony

Gary, a blend of professional and hippie, with long hair that he slicked back into a ponytail while working, but let hang loose outside the office, represented Greg, the husband. Although he always dressed professionally for work, he usually wore brightly tie-dyed socks that occasionally peeked out from below his suit pants, and wilder, more upbeat ties than his colleagues.

Greg and Carol's twelve-year marriage had produced an eight-year-old daughter who was the center of both of their universes. Greg was a tall man, still slender in his early forties with dark hair prematurely silver at the temples. He had a weary look that Pauline hoped would fade once the divorce process was finished.

Greg hated his job. Although it ate away at his soul, inch by inch, he remained in it because, when Kayla had been born, he and Carol had agreed that she would stay home to be a full-time mom. While Greg's position in finances paid quite well, for him, it was "wretched."

When Greg and Carol met, she had been a graphic artist. Theirs was a fairytale story of "opposites attract."

She was a petite, trim brunette. She kept her enthusiastically curly red hair short, so that it wouldn't interfere when she painted. She had taken up watercolors when Kayla was four, and not as underfoot as she had been as a toddler, and when it became apparent that she was unlikely to get pregnant again.

They had both imagined that this would be her outlet, just a hobby. But when Kayla was six and began attending school seven hours a day, Carol pursued her art in earnest. This was her passion, and she discovered that she had true talent. At first, she donated a few pieces here and there to school fundraisers and the like. Then people began searching her out to place special orders; dealers approached her about producing more as demand for her work increased.

In the process, she became active in the arts community where they lived. She taught classes, and there were a number of galleries that were interested in promoting her. She was often asked to attend events where she met other artists. Before she knew it, she had fallen in love with another painter.

She fought her preoccupation with this other man. Initially, she and Greg pursued couples therapy for quite some time. But Carol and her artist had too much in common, and all she had previously known with Greg was that "opposites attract." Now she had discovered how exciting it was to have so much substance to discuss with her romantic interest every day. Eventually, she realized that she wanted a life with this man, and asked Greg for a divorce.

Greg was terribly hurt, and very angry. He felt that he had sacrificed every possibility of finding a fulfilling career because he had agreed that Carol could stay home to care for Kayla, and now she had abandoned him. He hated his job, and he was going to lose the family for whom he had remained in that miserable job. But, because protecting Kayla from any divorce blowback was so important to both of them, he agreed to try the collaborative process.

The team convened for the first meeting at Gary's office because of its central location. Even though Pauline had had several cases with him previously, she had never been to his office. Had this collaboration occurred today, his conference room would likely have been a peaceful environment, with plush chairs, soothing music, and calming colors, much like Pauline's. But in the 1990s, Gary's office afforded them a standard, big-law-firm conference room furnished with an over-sized boardroom-style table and a congregation of leather office chairs. The large table and minimal decorations created a cold, formal atmosphere. To create a sense of intimacy, the four team members huddled together at one end of the table.

Gary was a younger guy, with more forward-thinking ideas regarding collaborative practice. He tried to put Greg and Carol at ease by offering them cold and hot beverages and placing bowls of salty snacks within easy reach. He dimmed the lights a degree so that the room appeared less intimidating. He even took off his jacket, loosened his tie, and rolled up his sleeves, in an effort to render the setting less intense. Pauline appreciated his efforts, but made a note to offer to host the remaining meetings at her more warm and welcoming office.

Although Greg had accomplished a great deal of processing during their couples' therapy, he still exuded grief and misery during the team meetings. But he must have reserved his emotional displays for meetings with Gary or his therapist; Pauline rarely observed anything more than quiet tears, which Carol studiously and expressionlessly ignored. The team meetings were, for the most part, business-like and focused on problem-solving the divorce issues, both financial and legal.

The most crucial and most difficult topic for discussion was alimony. How much would Carol be able to earn as an artist? Was there any other occupation in which she could earn more? How much would Greg be required to subsidize her while she fashioned her new livelihood? Most difficult to discuss, would she re-marry and, if so, how quickly? Thanks to the lawyers, with their substantial experience in marital matters, this led to a complicated and angst-filled debate of what Kayla's relationship would be with the artist in Carol's life, and, if not with him, then with any other significant other.

Ultimately, it became clear that Greg would be forced to continue at his vile job, supporting her, while Carol would be able to move forward in her new life.

Nevertheless, the couple was committed to working out their dissolution of marriage issues, and they did. Gary and Pauline were supportive and suggested solutions to many of the issues that were raised that might never have occurred to either Greg or Carol. The lawyers limited full team meetings to two hours each, to reduce the participants' emotional exhaustion. The process consumed only three full team meetings; during that time, there were several lawyer-client meetings off-line, but, all told, Greg and Carol resolved their divorce issues within three months of retaining their attorneys.

The marital settlement agreement had been drafted. Both attorneys had reviewed it with their clients and had suggested and agreed upon revisions. Four copies had been printed. The lawyers scheduled a final meeting at Pauline's office to execute the documents.

They met in Pauline's conference room, an intimate space with a round table circled by four overstuffed chairs. Several comfortable-looking armchairs crouched in the corners of the room, accompanied by small side tables and overseen by standing lamps. Pauline's assistant had baked Tollhouse cookies, and there was even a bottle of champagne chilling in the corner.

The clients sat across from each other, both looking very unhappy, but for different reasons. They had met with their lawyers immediately prior to this final get-together and they knew what was supposed to take place. The lawyers sat across from each other, a little nervous that the deal might fall apart at the last minute, but optimistic because of their clients' progress during the collaborative process.

Pauline and Gary alternated reading sections of the clients' marital settlement agreement word-for-word. At the end of each segment, the reader asked both participants whether they approved it. The clients each concurred aloud that they understood and agreed to the provisions of the document. All four copies of the MSA were then passed around the table and executed by all four team members, the lawyers as well as the clients.

Once the settlement agreement was signed, the procedure was concluded. There would be a five-minute "uncontested" hearing before a judge to obtain the final judgment approving the settlement agreement that the state required to recognize the dissolution of their marriage. Only one of the participants would need to attend that.

From experience, the lawyers recognized that more was required to recognize this life-changing event. They congratulated the clients for working so hard to find solutions with which they could both live, even if they weren't perfect for each one of them. They popped the champagne, passed around the fresh cookies, and Pauline and Gary each made a congratulatory speech, as was their wont. Pauline talked about how impressed she was that the participants had put the best interests of their daughter ahead of their own desires and needs. And Gary focused on Greg when he talked about the fresh start, the new life that each client could anticipate, to which each should look forward. Pauline hoped that Greg could hear what Gary was trying to tell him.

Then, unexpectedly, Carol asked if she would be allowed to say something. Everyone said, "Yes, of course." (The collaborative process belongs to the participants, after all.) She drew her shoulder bag out from under her chair and pulled out what seemed to be a form of altar cloth, an exquisitely embroidered turquoise fabric that she smoothed out ceremonially on the table between herself and Greg, connecting them to each other. It looked like something she might have made herself. She retrieved a decorative teal-colored plate and a matching four-inch tall handmade candle, which she placed carefully on the plate. She produced a squat little pot of incense which she placed in front of the plate. She then lit both the candle and the incense. (They were in Northern California, after all.) It was clear that she had given much thought to this ceremony.

During this process, Greg appeared completely perplexed, his eyebrows lifted nearly into his hairline. Pauline and Gary simply waited.

Then she reached around the candle and the incense, across the table, and secured Greg's hands in her own.

"Greg," she began, taking a deep breath, "this has been very, very difficult for you, and I can't tell you how much I appreciate everything you've done to work with me through this process. More than that," she continued, tears filling her eyes, "I am so very, very sorry for everything I have done to hurt you. I know that I have wounded you immensely, and you don't deserve that." By this time, Pauline could not help tears from spilling down her own cheeks. And she was not alone; Gary and Greg were both silently crying. "You are a wonderful man and a great father. I will always love you, and I hope that we will always be friends and that, some day, I can make this up to you. But for now, I just want you to know that I never meant to hurt you. I am so, so sorry. I just wanted you to know that. I thought it was important that I tell you that and that our attorneys bear witness to this. Thank you. Thank you for a wonderful marriage, for a marvelous child, and for a peaceful divorce. Thank you for the opportunity to pursue happiness differently than we imagined we would when we were young."

Greg reacted slowly. First, he sighed, deeply, his chin quivering with emotion. Knowing the stress that he had been under all these months, and the sadness in his eyes, Pauline was certain that he would break down and begin to sob. But he did not. They all waited.

Finally, Greg said, "Carol, thank you for that. It means the world to me to know that our twelve years together weren't wasted, and I know that Kayla has a wonderful mother in you. That will never change, no matter how angry I am that our marriage has ended. This process has helped me to appreciate that. I believe that you were never looking for someone else and I promise to try to be your friend, no matter what."

For the first time, Pauline felt that Greg would soon be able to begin the process of healing.

Had the clients litigated their issues, it is unlikely that Carol would ever have made her apology. Nor would Greg have accepted it.

About the Author

Joryn Jenkins is an attorney with 35 years of experience in the courtroom. She focuses her practice on courtless divorce at *Open Palm Law*, in Tampa, Florida. Ms. Jenkins received her B.A. from Yale University and her J.D. from Georgetown University Law Center. She is a former editor of *The Family Law Commentator* and the former editor-in-chief of both *The Federal Lawyer* and *The Bencher*, magazines with national circulations. She is the author of *Florida Civil Practice Motions* (LEXIS LAW PUBLISHING) and *The Stepmother's Cookbook*.

Joryn represented one of the spouses in the first *pro bono* collaborative divorce completed in Florida. She has appeared on Fox 13, ABC Action News, NBC 8, and Bay News 9, as well as on radio on *The Sam Sorbo Show*, *Legally Speaking*, *Ask the Dom*, and *Social Media Today*. She has also been featured in *The Tampa Bay Times*, *The Tampa Tribune*, and *The World of Collaborative Practice* e-zine, all on the subject of collaborative practice and divorce.

Joryn founded the *Cheatwood American Inn of Court* in 1988, and served in its leadership until after her presidency in 2001. She also founded the *Coordinating Council of Florida Inns* in 1989, and served on the American Inn of Court Board of Trustees from 1991 until 1997.

In 2001, Joryn received the *A. Sherman Christensen Award*, the only award then bestowed in the courtroom of the United States Supreme Court, for ethics, professionalism, and civility.

The Federal Bar Association bestowed its highest honor, *The President's Award*, on Joryn in 1997.

Joryn's Next Book

War or Peace explores the core principles of collaborative divorce, and illustrates those precepts with true stories of divorce. If you are interested in a more in-depth examination of the more complex issues raised in real collaborative divorce cases, look for Joryn's next book, *... and I Never Saw My Father Again (The Divorce Court Effect)*.

Made in the USA
Lexington, KY
25 July 2015